HOW FAITH AND FUN CAN MAKE YOUR MARRIAGE AND BUSINESS…

COMPLETE

KATE DESANTIS

Printed in the United States of America

ISBN: 978-1-939237-59-0

Published by Suncoast Digital Press, Inc.

Sarasota, Florida, USA

Contents

1: The Business of Marriage 1

2: Time to Get Real 29

3: Reprioritizing Your Life 53

4: No-Work Zones 81

5: I'll Do My Job, You Do Yours 113

6: Keys to Communication 149

7: A New Kind of Commitment 165

8: Letting Go 179

9: Reflect, Reset, Give Back 201

Diagrams

Diagram 1.0: Mismatched Expectations 13

Diagram 2.0: Stress Issues 51

Diagram 3.0: Priorities 55

Diagram 4.0: Marriage Boundaries 111

Diagram 5.0: Job Responsibilities 121

Diagram 6.0: Love Languages 163

Diagram 7.0: Matching Strengths and Responsibilities 185

Diagram 8.0: Finding Opportunities to Serve 206

And let steadfastness have its full effect,that you may be perfect and complete, lacking in nothing.

—James 1:4

Success is being in charge of your lifestyle
and creating something you're proud of,
surrounded by people you love.

Troye Sivan, Musician and Digital Star

Preface

Owning a business is hard. Owning a business with your spouse is *really* hard.

I have lived my life surrounded by family businesses and have seen the struggles and rough edges that always seem to perforate and define them. My parents, over the years, owned seven companies together and I watched as it taxed their marriage and constantly pushed and pulled at our family life. My sister and brother-in-law own a business together and live with the pressures of success daily. My husband and I own a business together and, interestingly, through our consulting work, we seem to continuously attract other married business owners who are in the midst of familiar challenges. Over time, I have seen the same themes; communication problems, missed expectations, and role confusion create a messy soup of a relationship that needs to be solid and grounded. On the other hand, these challenges are not insurmountable. I know first-hand that you can feel confident and effective in your roles as wife, mother, and business co-owner. And I know this can be profoundly satisfying, wonderful, and can provide a sense of feeling "complete."

As I prayed for all the people I knew who struggled with these issues, God revealed His plan for me. It became crystal clear to me that I needed to offer my own hard-won wisdom and encouragement to others, and that the most impactful way to accomplish that would be to write a book. (Gulp!) The fear set in and I didn't feel qualified, but God gently reminded me of my life verse: *"Praise be to the God and Father of our Lord Jesus Christ, the Father of compassion and the God of all comfort, who comforts us in all our troubles, so that we can comfort those in any trouble with the comfort we ourselves receive from God."* 2 Corinthians 3-4. When empathy is paired with action, great things happen. This book is my action.

As we walk this path together, there are times when I will sound like a friend talking to you over a cup of coffee. There will be times when I sound like a mama letting you know you've got to stop the madness. Why? Because both are components to being a good friend and coach. Expect to be stretched as you go through this process. Expect to grow and flourish, too.

This is about you taking back your life and living it with intentionality. This is about prioritizing your life and making decisions based on those priorities alone. It's about reaching out to each other in understanding rather than condemnation. This is about becoming complete. I want you to find yourself again. I want you to revive your love for each other and remember why it was you got married in the first place. By the end of our journey together, you will have acquired a blueprint for working and living together in harmony rather than discord. My prayer is that you will be empowered to design and live your life, from here on out, confident in your roles and literally inspired by your relationship.

"This is the true joy in life, the being used for a purpose recognized by yourself as a mighty one; the being a force of nature instead of a feverish, selfish little clod of ailments and grievances complaining that the world will not devote itself to making you happy.

I am of the opinion that my life belongs to the whole community, and as long as I live it is my privilege to do for it whatever I can.

I want to be thoroughly used up when I die, for the harder I work the more I live. I rejoice in life for its own sake. Life is no 'brief candle' for me. It is a sort of splendid torch which I have got hold of for the moment, and I want to make it burn as brightly as possible before handing it on to future generations."

—*George Bernard Shaw*

If I have the gift of prophecy and can fathom all
mysteries and all knowledge, and if I have a faith
that can move mountains,
but do not have love, I am nothing.

1 Corinthians 13:2

Introduction

"I don't want you to fall," my dad said to me as he gripped my arm in the crook of his. I looked up at this man who had held me tight all my 28 years and then looked down the stone path that led me to my soon-to-be husband. He waited in his tuxedo, smiling nervously and trying valiantly not to fidget. He was surrounded by everyone that meant the most to us, dressed in their very best. The wild array of flowers spilled out of the surrounding garden as if craning for a better view. I smiled inside. I was watching a vision come true.

"I won't fall, Dad. It'll be okay," I assured him.

"I'm going to hold on until I have to give you away. Got it?" he asked, getting misty-eyed for the first time in this whole wedding whirlwind.

"Got it," I said, trying to fight back my own tears. "Let's do this."

I have thought back to that moment thousands of times. I think about how prophetic it was when Dad warned me of the rocky path and promised, as God does, to hold on tight. The path of matrimony may be well-worn, but that doesn't make it smooth. What would I have done at my wedding if I had tripped on the hem of my gown, or on the uneven, stony ground? Just what you would have done—flamed red in embarrassment, asked for help from my dad, and then gotten myself back up and walking toward the alter. That, in a nutshell, has been our experience of marriage. We have tripped and even fallen several times. We have needed that firm hand of God to pick us up and dust off our knees so that we could try again.

Does the passion of new love and wedded bliss remain reliable enough to steady a marriage through shaky times? It was inconceivable to us during the romantic-love phase that we could ever feel anything but passionate bliss. The touch, sound, smell, and even presence of new love releases what are called the "love hormones," like dopamine and oxytocin, into our system. These give us a euphoric sense of connection and love, of power, as if we have immunity and are indestructible.

But it changes. Love goes from a blazing inferno to a low burn. Challenges that come with long-term partnerships test the couple's bond, faith, and resilience. We would all agree that marriage is a type of partnership. It has legal and societal rules for acceptable behaviors, ways to relate to one another inside the partnership, and to the world outside of the marriage. You see, the day you get married is just like the launch of a business. You are in a partnership where decisions must be made, money must be managed, planning must take place, and strategy must be discussed. These are not easy-breezy discussions. They are ripe with opportunities for "philosophical differences," i.e., arguments.

You might be against any type of debt, while your husband feels that cars shouldn't count as "real" debt. He may want to sell the house and travel the world the minute the kids go off to college, while you want to keep the house as a safe haven during school breaks. You may not believe in spanking, but he believes it's a biblical, effective discipline tool. How do these differences get resolved? Or how long can they go unresolved without the walls caving in? United you stand, divided you fall.

Does anyone really grasp the enormity of the marriage step before they say "I do"? Maybe not, or it would be too intimidating! By joining in matrimony, you are also combining your home, family, social, and financial structures "until death do us part." In essence, there isn't one area of your life that marriage doesn't impact, short-term and long-term.

Adding a business to the mix compounds the problems, doubles the challenges, and skyrockets the probability of disagreements in a marriage. When both the husband and wife are involved in the business, you really heat up the game and bring on the opportunities for an "interesting" marriage. Never boring, that's for sure. If you and your spouse have expanded your relationship into a business partnership, this book is for you.

Your marriage is the firm foundation on which you build your actual business partnership. If you have bad habits from your marriage partnership, they are sure to follow you to work every single day. If you haven't mastered money management, guess what? Your business is bound to struggle financially. If the two of you avoid conflict like the plague, unresolved issues will fester and infect your marriage and your company. If your parenting differences are a constant topic, employee management will be equally problematic. Owning a business is hard. Owning a business with your spouse is really hard. There are many,

many mistakes to avoid that I want to share with you, as well as some amazing tools that will help you succeed, BOTH in your business and in your marriage. It is my honor and passion to share these with you in this book.

I assembled Bible verses, personal experiences, lessons learned, life-changing books and workshops, my best heartfelt advice, and encouragement to build this book with you, a married business owner, always in mind. I hope that these lift you up and help you to dream about what is possible for your partnership.

I pray that reading this book will be like attending a transformative workshop for you and your husband. Making your dreams happen takes work and you will find ways to "make it happen" at the end of each section. Some assignments take moments, others may take an hour or more. The discussions, reflections, and activities will make this a personal experience for you. The value from completing them will be worth your time and effort, I promise. This is one of those times when the benefits you receive correlate to your commitment to get value; so, for the sake of your marriage, business, and self, give this your 100% effort.

Although many people have said that this book brings value to both men and women, I wrote it especially for the weary wife and mama that's doing everything she can to keep this life going. I wrote it for the experienced and driven business woman who has grand dreams and high expectations of herself, but always feels as if she's falling short. I wrote it to the woman who is seeking God's heart and trying to live out His love in every way. You are all those things and more. Your strength, your kindness, and your drive knit together to make something that is uniquely you.

Please know that my husband and I are far from perfect. This is not a book written from a high horse. We have had our fair share of troubles and I have always believed that transparency has power. Knowing our journey and the journey of others we have coached and loved can serve as a reminder that many have walked this path, fallen, and then risen up in His grace and forgiveness. Keep your eyes on Jesus and his amazing plans for you and your spouse.

I am praying this for you every day:

My dear sweet Lord, I lift up each and every person that you have chosen to read this book. I wrap them in your loving arms and ask the Holy Spirit to fill their souls and open their hearts. I ask the words that they need to hear leap from the page and give them the tools they need to succeed in their faith, their marriage and their business. Overwhelm them with your blessings, God.

In Jesus' mighty name, Amen.

1

The Business of Marriage

Love is patient, love is kind;
love does not envy or boast;
it is not arrogant or rude.
It does not insist on its own way;
it is not irritable or resentful;
it does not rejoice at wrongdoing,
but rejoices with the truth. Love bears all things,
believes all things, hopes all things,
endures all things.

1 Corinthians 13:4-7

If I learned anything from being the child of serial entrepreneurs, it's that a marriage and a family can be run like a business. That may seem odd—business and love may seem like oil and water. I propose to you that the opposite is true. Relationships crave clarity, direction and mutual understanding. As you read this book, you are going to begin the process of pouring the foundation for your marriage and family. You are going to establish a shared philosophy that will take time to cure but will be solid as a rock once it is complete. It will be the place you go to resolve differences, make decisions, and discuss potential problems before they arise. Let's get proactive.

Storyboarding is a tool that is often associated with filmmaking, but it also translates very well into business and personal decision-making. My parents were introduced to it in the mid-80s by a business consultant, Bob Jacobson. He learned the method from Mike Vance, who had also taught it to the executives at Disney. It's dynamic, fast-paced and powerful. This simple tool changed the trajectory of my parents' home health care agency and took them from $500,000 in revenue to $7 million in a few short years.

My parents had used storyboarding to develop a philosophy for their business and defined expectations about everything from employees to mistakes and communication. My mom decided to bring this tool home and we used it to develop the "Heim Family Philosophy." She wanted a highly visible way to communicate the morals, values, and expectations of our family. My parents created the first draft and then called a family meeting to share it with us.

"This is a list of everything we believe in. Daddy and I have spent a lot of time thinking this through, but we need your input, too," my mom said.

Items on the list included topics like friendship and teachers—the headings were categories of our lives that felt real and personal. I remember feeling this enormous responsibility to get this right. "How about, 'Sisters can't interrupt when we have friends over?'"

Mom smiled and said, "Great! Let's write it down."

I felt a surge of excitement, of validation, and as if my voice mattered in our family. That was all the motivation I needed to get hooked on this transformative tool.

The philosophy board was hung prominently in our hallway and my parents used it regularly as a reminder of who we are, how we behave, and what we believe in. We walked by it daily and read the lists absentmindedly. Phrases like, "We always tell the truth," and "Bad planning on your part does not constitute an emergency on mine" became part of our family vernacular and embedded into our hearts and minds.

If we strayed from these core beliefs and standards, Dad or Mom would bring us back to the board and say, "This is who you want to be. What choices can you make to get back on track?" We took time to evaluate and listen to their suggestions because we didn't feel attacked, just held accountable. My parents hadn't announced a huge list of rules, they had invited us to decide the kind of people we wanted to be. A simple wall poster became a powerful compass, always there to guide our steps in the right direction.

Your philosophy will be equally as powerful for you as a couple. How many times do you find yourself arguing over the same things? This forces you to agree in black and white. It allows you to work through it when you aren't in the middle of a stressful situation and focus on the big picture. Clarity has power. Simply knowing what you stand for as a couple helps you feel united in life's journey and keeps both of you on the right track.

Make it Happen (60 Minutes)

Now it's your turn. Let's build your philosophy. Don't worry if your children are still very young. Even children too young to read will grasp the concept quickly if the conversation is set up properly. Their innocent insights will become keepsakes in the years to come.

Storyboarding opens up thinking by engaging all the five senses. Here's your supply list:

- Scented markers and foam board
- Multi-colored sticky notes
- Food! (sweets and something salty does the trick)
- Clay or stress balls for the kinesthetic one

The rules are straightforward but can be difficult to follow. Habits are hard to break!

1. **No Criticism:** "Everyone knows that instant judgment is the enemy of creativity," writes Edward de Bono in *Serious Creativity.* Your family will clam up as soon as one person gets criticized. Remember, you are asking them to step out and share something very personal. Ideas are part of our uniqueness; it takes trust and willingness to be vulnerable to share them. It is natural to automatically AGREE/DISAGREE with what another person says, but in this exercise, you keep those thoughts to yourself and only say, "Yes! What else?" Be firm and clear about this rule. If you hear judgment creeping in, interrupt and say, "Ideas only, please!" They may just find a way to turn their concern into a fresh concept.

2. **No Discussion:** Nothing slows down brainstorming more than elaboration. Every meeting has that person who over-explains (I know you already have someone in your head! I won't tell.) But this is not a typical meeting—this should feel like a round of that old game show Password. One idea per sticky note. No details. For those of you sweating about this prospect, know that there will be a phase for details. Storyboarding sessions are not that place.

You will be the organizer and facilitator of the first storyboarding session. Your job is to lead the session and ask questions to provoke out-of-the-box thinking. Be sure everyone participates. With practice, you will learn how to be encouraging vs. insistent. For example, I learned that if someone says, "I don't know," I can elicit a response by saying, "Okay. And if you DID know, what would you say?"

Make the following header cards and stick them along the top of your foam board. I have listed an example of a completed category to get your wheels turning.

- About Parenting
- About Marriage
- About Money
- About God
- About Secrets
- About Time
- About Sex (Don't let this one scare you. It's necessary. You can have one version about your relationship and one for your beliefs about your children's sexual conduct.)
    - Kid Example: Only adults can really explain it
    - Adult Example: It only happens within the bounds of our marriage
- About Other Peoples' Things

- About Parents (This pertains to your parents as well as the way you want to be treated as parents.)
- About Mistakes
- About People

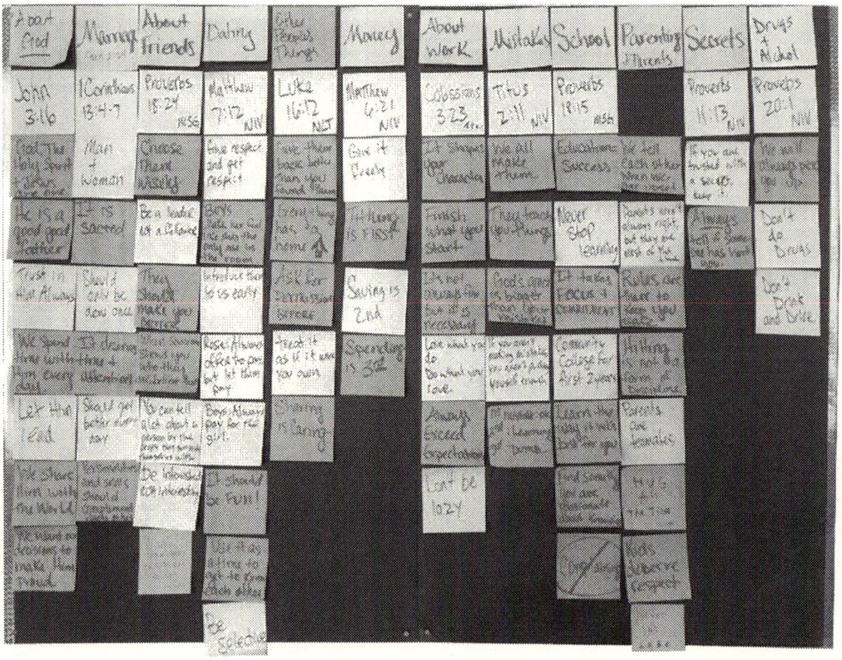

Here is a real-life example...my family's!

You'll want to free the room of electronic distractions. Put the phones, iPads, etc. in a basket outside the room. This is important and should be treated like a meeting with your best client. Set the stage with something like this: "We brought you here tonight to define who we are and who we want to be. Daddy and I want you to know what we expect of you and we want to know what you expect of us. We've already listed some things out that are important to us but we need your input, too. This will become an accountability tool. That means when any of us mess up, we will use this as a reminder that we can be better. Our family is a team and we are going to work together to help keep each other on track."

"We are going to use a fun tool called storyboarding and it's the same thing they used to design Disney World. There are no wrong answers. I will ask you a question and you just shout out what you think. By the end, we'll know exactly what's important to us as a family. Ready?"

The organizer (you, in this case) will begin with warm-up question like, "What animals are the cutest?" Everyone will shout out their answers and write them on sticky notes. This helps free up their thinking so that the hard stuff comes out a bit easier. Once you have filled the category, you can move on to the actual content of the brainstorming. (Note: my children are on the younger side, so my examples may not fit your family, but the exercise and process is adaptable and does work for any size family with any-aged members.)

Choose one header at a time and ask, for example, the simple question, "What do we believe about parenting?"

No answers are wrong at this stage. Just shout out an answer as you write it on the sticky note. Think of how you prefer to discipline, what your end goals are for your kids, or things that you want to teach them as they grow. You may even want to include verses under each category. It's a beautiful way of bringing scripture to life.

Here are example results in the Parenting category:

- We "raise them up in the way they should go."
- We discipline privately.

- Yelling and hitting hurt. Don't do it.

- We are raising disciples.

- Kids deserve respect, too.

- We present a united front to our kids.

- We are a family that plays together.

- We build them up rather than tear them down.

Continue with each category until you have at least four cards under each one. Read through them and find out if there are any that you disagree with. Discuss them. Rewrite them once you've reached some sort of compromise. Remember, this board is an accountability partner and these are the standards you must follow. Make sure you are behind them wholeheartedly.

Put the board up in a prominent location. You will find yourself reading it all the time and the words will become part of the fabric of your life together. (My sister and I can't have a tough discussion without one of those phrases being said by one of us!)

As with other peaks of achievement in life, time erodes what you build. Regular communication MUST be your priority.

Make it Happen (20 Minutes)

1. **Weekly Business of Marriage Meetings**

   Every good partnership checks in to see how things are progressing. Marriage is no different. Schedule a time once a week to go over the most pressing business. Are the kids' pick-ups and drop-offs scheduled? How are you doing with your budget for that week? Any meetings or social obligations that you should know about?

And, most importantly, remember to check in with each other about "ways of *being*," not just "what we are *doing*." For example, ask, "Is there anything I neglected to do this week that you have not told me about?" or "Do you have any unresolved upsets?" or "How did I show up as your committed partner this week?"

Like any efficient and productive meeting, your Business of Marriage meeting needs a brief, written agenda. There are many reasons this will be helpful. First, each of you will know ahead of time what to expect. Especially when this practice is new, you don't want either of you to feel apprehensive about an unusually formal meeting (one that is scheduled ahead of time and treated like an important appointment). Your agenda will simply serve as a checklist, a guide to remind you what to cover so nothing gets neglected. Other topics may come up, of course, but you should always have your agreed-upon basic agenda to follow.

What do you think will be the best way to always have it handy? Perhaps one of you already uses their smart phone for utilitarian purposes such as note-taking and scheduling reminders, so the BOM meeting agenda can be stored on the phone, which is probably going to be handy no matter when or where you meet. On the other hand, both people should be responsible, so if the other person doesn't like to use their phone, they can laminate a credit-card sized checklist and keep it in their wallet. Again, this would probably be handy at any time, and it's smart for both people to have the BOM list, just in case. One husband I know set up a composition notebook and brings it to each BOM meeting, which gives him the opportunity to keep meeting notes all in one place. (It is still a good idea to also have the agenda list in your phone or wallet.)

EXAMPLE:

BOM MEETING — OUR AGENDA

Schedule

- Any evenings out this week?
- Dentist or other appointments to work around?
- Pick-ups/drop-offs that need to be planned?
- Maintenance workers coming to the house?
- Trips or visitors coming up?

Budget

- Are we on track for our budgeting/spending?
- Any new spending plan items to discuss?
- Any new income items to discuss?
- Any irregular expenditures coming (repairs, travel, kids' activities, etc.)?

Check-In

- Did I neglect anything this week that you haven't told me about yet?
- Do we have anything unresolved between us?
- When did you feel my committed partnership this week?
- How can I make this upcoming week easier for you?

If there are major decisions to make or conflicts to resolve, turn to your philosophy. Are there clues there that can guide you? For example, if you have decided to be a debt-free household, financing a brand new car isn't in the cards for you. Perhaps a new savings account would be a better option as you save up for a nice but used car. Let the board serve as a reminder of previously agreed-upon decisions and take the emotion out of the conversation.

Some weekly meetings will be a piece of cake (they tend to get smoother and easier with practice). Some may take longer and even feel draining. Just as adversity builds personal character, working through difficult subjects together builds a stronger marriage. One huge advantage of weekly meetings is that the wrinkles that need ironing out can be addressed and resolved before they set in and become long-term issues. The key is to have the meeting, each and every week. A regularly scheduled day and time works best.

I know a couple that goes out to breakfast every Saturday to address the Business of Marriage. "It's our time to get through the boring stuff so that we can spend the rest of the week with aligned expectations," she shared with me. "Life has become a lot more fun."

How does Saturday morning look for you? Find a time that you and your spouse can at least have your first Business of Marriage meeting and schedule it now, before you continue reading. It's that important.

FANTASY VS. REALITY

I wish I could tell you that having a philosophy will make all of your troubles disappear but it's only the first step. Knowing expectations sometimes makes you more critical of your spouse when they fail to meet them. My mom said to me on my wedding day, "There will be some days that you say, 'I can't believe I got to marry this man!' There will be other days when you say, 'I can't believe I married this man.' Both are normal."

She's so right. Do you know what the number one cause of divorce is in our country? Unmet expectations. Let that sink in for a minute. It's not adultery or financial difficulties. It's the little interactions that occur in a marriage day after day that bring about the demise of a union.

Dane and I struggled with unmet expectations early in our marriage. We had both lived on our own for ten years. We had a right way and a wrong way to do everything. I remember having a full-out argument because he refused to buy an electric can opener. I had never used a manual one and I wasn't about to start then. It's almost embarrassing to admit!

To this day, I ask Dane what the weather is going be like because my dad watched The Weather Channel religiously. He was my personal meteorologist with up-to-the minute info whenever I asked. But Dane says every time, "Don't know. Check on your phone."

There were other differences that led to feelings of rejection and discouragement. He would cringe each time I cooked dinner for him because the kitchen looked like an atomic bomb went off afterward. You see, we have a deal that one of us cooks and the other cleans up. When he cooked, he would do dishes and wipe counters along the way.

I prefer to go with the flow and let the spices fall where they may. The dishes were taking him a solid half hour at 8 o'clock at night and he would say things like, "I hate it when you cook." I thought he hated my cooking but he just felt overwhelmed at having such a mess to clean up after a long day of work. We had different expectations.

You have your own expectations of your husband and he has expectations of you. Some are silly like my weather channel example, but some reach right down into your heart. You may have expected him to continue flirting with you or taking you on those amazing, romantic dates and that has all but faded. You may have expected criticism to be less present in your marriage and pray that his words will not cut so deep this time. You are not alone in this.

Mismatched Expectations

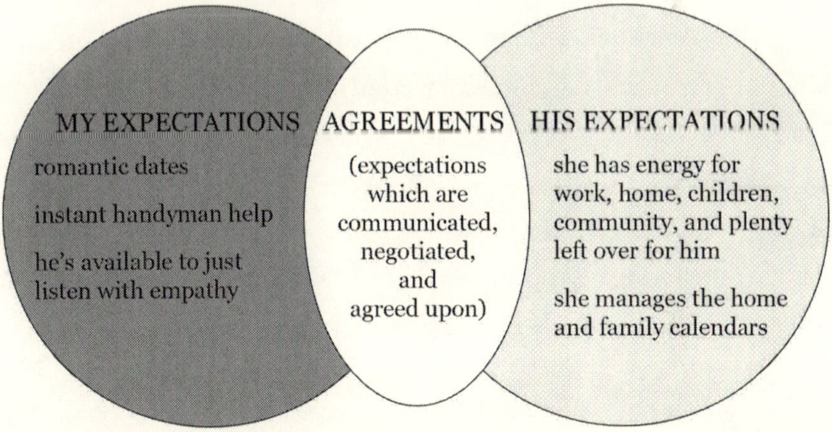

Diagram 1.0

"Being married exposes how much a husband and wife *do not know* about each other," writes Myles Munroe, author of *Purpose and Power of Love and Marriage*. "It is after the wedding when their less attractive and less appealing qualities show themselves. When that happens, it can be quite a shock."

Are the "less appealing" qualities of your spouse jumping into your mind right now? Write a few down—you're going to need them in a minute.

It's so easy to see where we want them to change. I was stuck in that place for a time, as well. It seemed that everything my husband did wasn't right. He didn't speak to the children kindly enough. He didn't talk to me enough. He was too critical of my choices. He loved me with devotion, but that meant he wanted me with him all the time.

These struggles deepened when we found out that my third pregnancy was high risk. My unborn baby girl was getting more anemic every day and the doctors were constantly weighing the risks of delivering her early to stop anemia vs. keeping me pregnant to fight the major complications that come with prematurity. Amidst all of this, my husband was presented with an out-of-state job offer. We were torn. I had always wanted our children to grow up surrounded by family. His expectation was that he would follow the road to success, wherever that may lead. That decision-making process had worked for him for so long, why wouldn't it work now? They were offering an outstanding financial package and the option to move quickly up the corporate ladder. He couldn't see a downside. I couldn't see an upside. We were at a nasty crossroads.

We tried to talk it through but the conversations felt more like boxing matches. We defended our corners fiercely and hurt each other more with each blow. Neither of us could see past winning the argument. I was broken inside. This man who was supposed to love and protect me was doing everything but keeping that promise. Or so I thought.

God knows our hearts and always has perfect timing. I was asked by a friend to attend a book study on *The Power of the Praying Wife* by Stormie Omartian. Dane and I had yet another argument before I left for the first meeting and let's just say I wasn't in the mood to be a praying wife. During the study, this section jumped off the page for me: "I Don't Even Like Him—How Can I Pray for Him?" writes Omartian. "Have you ever been so mad at your husband that the last thing you wanted to do was pray for him? So have I. It's hard to pray for someone when you're angry or he's hurt you. But that's exactly what God wants us to do. If He asks us to pray for our enemies, how much more should we be praying for the person with whom we have become one and are supposed to love?"

Talk about being at the right place at the right time; I felt as if the words were piercing me, or at least they were starting to penetrate my frustrated, negative attitude. I wanted to hear more.

"But how do we get past having an unforgiving and critical attitude?" the book study leader continued reading aloud. "The first thing to do is be completely honest with God. In order to break down the walls in our hearts and smash the barriers that stop communication, we have to be totally up-front with the Lord about our feelings. We don't have to 'pretty it up' for Him. He already knows the truth. He just wants to see if we're willing to admit it and confess it as disobedience to His ways."

These are some seriously powerful words of wisdom. The phrase, "… how much more should we be praying for the person with whom we have become one and are supposed to love?" struck me. The book study walked me through several prayers that reminded me over and over again that I needed to stop nagging and start praying. I needed to put my trust in God and stop believing that I held all the power. I'm not going to lie; some of the prayers I was asked to say felt like eating crow.

I realized I had let my negative thinking overtake my mind rather than praying for him to overcome those challenges. Pushing myself beyond my own limited thinking changed everything.

I prayed so hard for God to give Dane the opportunities he was seeking. I prayed that I would hear my husband, really hear him, when we talked. I prayed that I could trust God to lead us to live wherever He wanted us to live. I stopped fighting and started praying.

Three days later, out of nowhere, Dane sat me down and said, "I've decided we need to stay here. I don't want to uproot us during this stressful time. I want to do what's best for our family and so I've turned down the job offer." *Only God!*

I went into labor at the very last book study and those women that had lifted me up during a dark hour of my marriage held my hands and prayed all through those first contractions. I gave birth that night to a beautiful baby girl, grateful also for my new perspective about what kind of wife I should teach my daughter to become.

Make it Happen (5 Minutes)

1. Refer to the list of "less appealing" qualities you noted earlier in this chapter, or write down the ones that are top of mind, i.e., things that disappoint you about your spouse. I want you to take a few minutes to pray over these. God loves you so much. He already knows what you are going through, but He wants to hear it from you. It's not easy to be that vulnerable, even with our Lord, but it's the first step toward knowing what your heart is hungering for. It's the first step toward receiving the unconditional love that you deserve. Complain to the Lord like you would to your best friend. Be real about your frustrations and pain. Give

your relationship to God and ask that your husband is given the complete protection of the full armor of God to overcome those challenges. Do it every day if you need to. I promise He hears you and I know from experience that miraculous things will happen because if it.

2. We've all grown up with an idea of our own happily-ever-after and all experienced the steep learning curve that comes with saying "I do." There's a reason 1 Corinthians is read at most weddings. We need that verse in our hearts from the beginning to be able to handle all the challenges that will surely come.

   Did you have someone read 1 Corinthians 13:4-7 on your wedding day? I believe it is a beautiful version of God's expectations of us as husbands and wives. We heard a sermon once that encouraged us to replace the word "love" with "I." How else can love live but through us? Read through this modified version and thank God for helping you embody these traits.

   - I am patient and kind.
   - I do not envy or boast.
   - I am not arrogant or rude.
   - I do not insist on getting my own way.
   - I am not irritable or resentful.
   - I do not rejoice at wrongdoing but rejoice in truth.
   - I bear all things, believe all things, hope all things, endure all things.

Use this list as your own personal standards of performance. No one is perfect—that's why grace is given—but do your best to live up to the promises you made on your wedding day.

FROM 50/50 TO 100/100

Now what about him? Doesn't he have to step up his game? Shouldn't he be praying for you and trying to live out 1 Corinthians 13? Absolutely. But not in the way you might think.

There's a misleading concept that permeates our society. We hear it said that marriage is a partnership and that each person should give 50/50. It seems sensible at first glance. But how do you know if your spouse has truly met you halfway? Is it your halfway or their halfway? When we only give half, we spend so much time measuring what they've done against some invisible yardstick. And we are setting them up for failure. Actually, the 50/50 mindset sets you up for failure, too.

I remember my parents having an argument about who changed the toilet paper roll the most times. Time and time again she would go into the bathroom only to find an empty roll and it started to drive her crazy. "Paul!!!" she yelled from her awkward position in the bathroom. "How hard is it to change the !#$% toilet paper roll?!" (My mom is a wonderfully colorful character.)

My dad shot up from his newspaper to defend himself. "I change it every time it runs out!" He stopped to think for a moment, defenses rising, and took it a step further by challenging her. "I'll bet I change it even more than you do!"

Challenge accepted, she thought. "Oh yeah? Then save every one you change for a month. We'll see who has changed more rolls!"

The best part of the story is that they actually followed through on this ridiculous challenge. They counted them at the end of the month and found that my mom had changed three times as many toilet paper rolls as he had. Chagrined, my dad giggled at himself. Being right had seemed so important a month ago, but now the whole thing just seemed silly.

Worth the time? Probably not. Funny? Definitely. We can get so competitive about who has done more that we seek to prove ourselves through a myriad of different ways. FamilyLife Ministry describes the phenomenon this way: "Acceptance is based upon performance—you do your part, and I'll do mine."

Here's the problem with this approach. We only want to give to our spouse when we are happy with them. We only reach out and do something loving or thoughtful when they "deserve it." Unfortunately, we are always falling short. We forget to change the toilet paper, we lose our patience with our kids, we make a snide comment about dinner not being up to par. Those little things build up. And then something big happens. Something goes terribly wrong; you enter into a crisis. There's a medical emergency, a major decision you couldn't seem to agree on, a sudden loss of income, or all of the above. Life erupts and suddenly you are left trying to reassemble the pieces.

If you enter into a major conflict with a heart full of resentment and anger, it will overflow and cause this incredibly stressful situation to feel bigger than life. Suddenly this person you love has turned into someone you can't even look in the eye. You feel your anger provoked by every word they speak. Intimacy shuts down.

Giving 100% means loving with all you have *in spite of* his shortcomings. Don't you want to be loved that way? I know I do. Someone has to take the first step. Someone has to come forward with Jesus' heart. We are all sinners saved by grace. It's time to extend that grace to your spouse, even if he doesn't deserve it. Because it's not about either of you being "deserving," it's about bringing forth love, over and over, in order to build and maintain a strong and fulfilling marriage.

Make it Happen (30 Minutes)

1. **Let Go of Resentment**

   You cannot give 100% if you are holding on to past disappointments. *Psychology Today* describes resentment as "the mental process of repetitively replaying a feeling, and the events leading up to it, that goads or angers us. We don't replay a cool litany of facts in resentment; we re-experience and relive them in ways that affect us emotionally, physiologically, and spiritually in very destructive ways."

   Notice the words, "affect us." It does not say that resentment affects the other person. It does not say that it is destructive to anyone but yourself. There's no need to set yourself on fire and hope the smoke bothers the other person. It will not happen. Only you have the power to take control of this negative spiral.

   Your feelings are real and they matter, especially to your spouse. But he cannot make a change or clarify a misunderstanding if you do not share those feelings with him. Pray about how to approach your spouse with the issues that are still alive in your heart. Start small. Maybe it bothers you that he doesn't return texts. Ask God to reveal to you your true needs. You may feel as if you are not a priority and his attentiveness would show more devotion to you. Once you've gotten to the feeling rather than the action, bring that to him. Be prepared to hear your role in the conflict and accept responsibility. We are encouraged in Colossians 3:13 to "bear with each other and forgive one another." That is not to say that this is an easy task, but God will help you through it. Give those grievances to Him and ask Him to help you let go of those feelings.

Once your feelings have been aired, you will be tasked with true forgiveness. Matthew West sings a beautiful praise song called, "Forgiveness" that I read as a prayer. The chorus speaks to what we are called to do as followers of Jesus.

> *Show me how to love the unlovable*
>
> *Show me how to reach the unreachable*
>
> *Show me how to do the impossible*
>
> *Forgiveness*

Jesus loves the unlovable. He reaches the unreachable. His acceptance isn't based on performance at all. He simply asks us to proclaim our belief in His life, death, and resurrection. Why? Because in life we are constantly falling into the darkness and being raised up again toward the light. He gives us endless grace. Sometimes that is exactly what we must do in our marriages. It's not about feeling happy or fulfilled all the time. It's about pressing through your anger and hurt and being the first one to ask for forgiveness. It's about giving 100% all the time, whether your spouse deserves it or not. Easy? Definitely not. Worth it? Always.

2. **Embrace Your Differences**

   Take a moment and hold your hands out in front of you. One hand represents you and the other, your spouse. Now press your fingers together and put your palms together like a child saying a bedtime prayer. Your hands are together with the appearance of oneness but they can easily be pulled apart, right? Now I want you to spread out your fingers and interlock your hands. Notice how each finger has a place. Where one has a hole, the other can fill it. The bond is stronger because of these differences. Your marriage is as well.

It's true that opposites attract; how ingenious that God designed it that way? Take a moment to think about things that drive you crazy and then reframe it as a difference to be thankful for. For example, my husband is very social. I love a little social life, but I prefer to be with people I know very well. For years his social butterfly mentality made me insane. I've decided, instead, to be thankful that he has brought so many beautiful people into my life. I have an entire community of people I "know very well" rather than just a few. Okay, now it's your turn. Create two columns on a piece of paper and list: "Things that drive me nuts:" on the left and "That helps me because:" on the right side. Example:

Things that drive me nuts:	**That helps me because:**
He's a perfectionist.	He helps me to be patient about the process of getting things right.
He always wants to be with people.	He grows our friendships and business contacts naturally and effortlessly.
He asks endless questions to get details I don't yet have (or sometimes even care about!).	He catches details I have missed (like that one time I forgot to book a hotel room for a trip!).

No one goes into a marriage believing there will be zero work involved. Well, this is part of the necessary "work" you must do to have a healthy marriage. Be willing to pause, notice your angst, and ask yourself to find the gift in the situation. "Seek, and you shall find."

3. **Keep Score**

   We are really good at keeping score. We note every time the dishes are not put away or the hedge still needs trimming when we've asked them to do it. What if you kept track of the opposite? I challenge you to keep a mental scorecard of things your husband does right. Each time you notice, let him know. Say something like, "I really appreciate you grabbing milk on your way home," and then smile. Accentuate the positive. It will do you both some good. When you train your mind to notice things to be happy about, you WILL be happier. It just works that way!

WHAT'S YOUR GOAL

My mom used to say to me, "Does that choice get you closer to or further from your goal?" If your goal is oneness with your spouse and oneness with God, you have to put his or her needs first. It may be built-in to think of oneself first, but with commitment and faith, it can get easier to focus on the other person and be less self-consumed.

If you are making dinner while simultaneously fielding homework questions while your husband checks email on his phone, spouting "did you" questions, you probably want to scream and yell and grab that phone and throw it in the pasta pot. Doesn't he see that you are in the middle of six other things?! Why doesn't he put down the phone and help with SOMETHING!? And yet, you are both being self-centered.

You are thinking about what you are dealing with and he is thinking about what he is dealing with. Neither of you are looking beyond your own personal situation. This never has a positive outcome. Approaching each other in love means rewriting our habits in a constructive way.

What if he said, "Looks like you could use some help. Let me help out with homework then I'll take a few minutes to check my email..."? What a gift! You would feel seen and cared about. You would want to give him the time to check his email because he took care of you.

What if you said to your husband, "I know there's a lot happening at the office. Why don't you take ten minutes to get through that and I'll keep the kids busy..."? He would feel seen and appreciated. He would feel so thankful that you get it, and be more likely to return to you and his family with his full attention and other-centered vs. self-centered attitude.

People immediately love this concept but may feel that it's far-fetched. They worry that if they do the work that their husbands will take it and run. There will not be any reciprocity. It's an "If I don't do it, no one will" kind of attitude. But truly I tell you, the opposite is true. The more loved you feel, the more willing you are to love. If you stay stuck expecting to receive before you give, it's like standing in front of a fireplace saying, "Okay, you give me fire, then I'll give you wood."

There's a Christian movie with Kirk Cameron called *Fireproof* that shows us this exact concept. The wife feels invisible and unloved and has completely checked out of the marriage. She moves, like a shadow, through their home, avoiding any conversation because even innocuous topics erupt into a fight. The husband is critical and angry and extremely defensive. He goes to his father and tells him he's done with the marriage. Over it. Finished. His father challenges him to wait 40 days, and then mails him a 40-day "Love Dare" booklet that adds one new way to love his wife each day: A bouquet of flowers, coffee made just the way she likes it, a phone call that tells her what she really means to him. At first, she rejects it. She isn't ready to trust this drastic change and, understandably, is skeptical of her husband's motives. He's awkward, unpracticed, and even inauthentic. But as those 40 days progress, her heart begins to open. His selfishness is revealed to him. He begins to want to meet her needs and fulfill her. She is once again open to receiving that love.

We know that relationships need to be fed, not starved, and that they can only be nourished with love and respect. Is this something you remember every single day? When a woman is loved and a man is respected, relationships flourish. She feels free to be who she is and he feels important and heard. Another way I've heard it explained is that "a woman wants to be cherished" and "a man wants to be admired." Let's talk about a few things that will help get you there.

Make it Happen (10 Minutes)

There are two questions that will change your dynamic. They stop the madness of feeling as if we have to be perfect at everything and anticipate our husband's every need. The answers to the questions give you a clear path to living for each other. Here they are:

1. **What Can I Do?**

   Ask your husband this question every day before the work day begins: "What can I do today to make your day easier?" The answer may surprise you. Maybe he just needs his lunch packed because his day is packed with meetings. Maybe he needs you to stop at the store on the way home from work because he has a craving for barbeque and would love to have that to look forward to all day. Say yes no matter what it is. You may need to move your schedule around to accommodate his request. Annoyance can creep in from time to time (you're busy too, I know!), but it's worth the shuffling in the end.

Now it's his turn to ask the question. Take a moment to think of something (but not mountain-sized!) on your to-do list that has been bugging you. I am sure there is something that you can't seem to fit in the jigsaw puzzle of the day. Share it with him and enjoy the rush of knowing someone has got your back. You really do have a partner in this life. You don't have to figure this all out on your own.

Note: Don't give up too quickly. Dane said he didn't need me to do anything for him the first month we tried this and then, suddenly, he started asking for a bit of help here and there. I picked up dry cleaning or made that call to the exterminator he had been putting off. It fulfills me to be able to do something I *know* he needs instead of just guessing what he might need. As the favors are asked and fulfilled, trust grows exponentially. Little things that are counted on soon add up and the marriage will feel more and more like a true partnership.

2. **What Matters to You?**

Do you really know your husband? Does he really know you? We tend to assume more than perhaps we should. I encourage you to become less presumptive and more curious.

I used to rush home from work to clean up the house before Dane got home. I knew what that would mean to me—I would feel so relieved that I didn't have all that work to do after a full day at the office. He never seemed to notice. Ever. I finally brought it up and he said, "Oh, I just thought you liked to do that when you got home." Um, no. No I don't.

It opened up a conversation about the top three things that matter to us each day. He said things I had never even considered. For example, he wanted the kids' toys out of the way so that he could park in the garage. I couldn't have guessed that in a million years. I told him it would be nice if he made coffee every morning. He always wakes up first and it's nice to have that ready when I get up. It seemed so easy for each of us to say yes to something that was no big deal to us, but such a difference-maker for the other person.

They were simple things and yet they have had a profound impact. When I pour that first cup of coffee in the morning, I feel heard. I feel loved. I know he's making it because I matter to him. I hope he feels the same way when he is able to squeeze his car in the garage between all the bikes and balls and scooters. We work each day to make each other's lives easier and those small gestures show love in a big way. Now it's your turn.

Spend a date night asking each other the top three things you can do *every day* to make them feel cared for or loved. Make a commitment to each other to do those things consistently.

2

Time to Get Real

You shall remember the LORD your God,
for it is he who gives you power to get wealth,
that he may confirm his covenant that he swore
to your fathers, as it is this day.

Deuteronomy 8:18

RELEASING THE PRESSURE

Married people have enough to argue about without introducing a company into the mix. Suddenly this entity that was supposed to bring you financial freedom, independence, and control has become an albatross around your neck. Business problems have a way of following you home, sitting with you at dinner, hanging out during your kid's bath time, and lingering over cocktails when you are supposed to be on a date with your husband. They are intrusive and persistent. They demand that you give them attention. The pressure is immense.

I knew all of this when Dane began talking about being a business owner. I had grown up with serial entrepreneurs as parents and the pitfalls were as ingrained in me as the successes. But I was determined that we would be different.

We spent a long year of praying and talking about what direction he should take when God brought him an opportunity. An elder from our church owned a business brokerage and he was looking for a partner. It seemed like the perfect way to begin. It was a partnership that would give Dane the training he needed before being completely on his own. We had enough savings to make it happen and so we took a leap of faith and bought into the firm.

Eighteen months into the partnership, Dane's partner needed out. We put the kids to bed, then closed ourselves in our bedroom for an impromptu planning session. We huddled over our personal and business financials trying to figure out how we could buy him out of his half of the company and keep our family afloat. We took turns being the emotional one (This feels so unfair!) and the logical one (There's nothing we can do about it. Let's just figure it out.) Finally, we came up with a second plan. One that felt bullet-proof.

Only our plan wasn't bullet-proof at all. One deal after another fell through. We would get close to a closing date and something crazy and unexpected would happen. We prayed hard for them to close. We asked family and friends to join us in praying for success but time and time again, we met failure and disappointment. We were running through our savings like water and it became this constant presence in our day-to-day life.

As the months passed, I felt my faith giving in to fear. I stood in my laundry room folding the endless pile of clothes when I felt hot tears stinging my cheeks. It felt hopeless. I felt lost. And so I called the one I knew would understand more than anyone, my sister. I can call her and know I will get a best friend and a business shark all in one package. You can't get better advice than that.

"Hey, Kate!" she said brightly.

I got straight to the point. "I can't do this. It's all running out! The money is running out! I don't have any control over any of it. I just have to watch it all happen day after day! I want to add a recurring revenue stream but he keeps saying he's not ready! When will he be ready?!" I sank down on the floor of the laundry room and continued to spew out all my frustrations until I ran out of steam. She listened quietly but I could hear her wheels turning.

"What does Dane think?" she asked, knowing the wisdom my husband always brings to the table.

"I've been trying to stay positive for him, you know? He's got so much on his plate right now!"

"Katie! You have to tell him what you need. It's okay to tell him you're afraid, maxed out, or needing a real plan B. His job is to protect you but he'll never be able to do his job if you don't tell him." I had cleared my own turmoil of thoughts enough that I could actually hear what she was saying now. I began to think about what I could do, not just about how bad things felt.

"And the recurring revenue idea is a good one," she continued. "You're on the right track. Don't give up, okay? Trust your instincts."

It was good advice. I had been so aware of his struggles that I had ignored my own. I had ignored that he was working much longer hours while I tried to juggle three children and our household. I had ignored that I needed to talk about something other than this business. I had ignored my fear so that I could be strong for him. If I had continued down that path, more and more resentment would have grown between us. That was the last thing I wanted for our marriage.

That night we put on a movie for the kids and opened a bottle of wine for us. We spent two straight hours talking and getting real about the emotional toll this was taking on both of us. The tears flowed and he was truly surprised to hear that I had been hiding so many anxieties and fears. We held each other and prayed for provision from God. We told Him we were living on His promise to "prosper you and not to harm you; plans to give you hope and a future" (Jeremiah 29:11). I felt understood for the first time in six months.

A study by the American Psychological Association (APA) found that, in a marriage, "the two most common stressors were work and money, and that stress causes irritability, anger, nervousness, and anxiousness. Those emotions carry into the home at the end of the work day."

Boy, do they ever! The one thing I've learned about negative emotions is that they grow at the speed of light. When you feel a tiny bit angry, every little thing fuels that fire inside. You end up saying things you don't mean and hurting the people you love the most. When you feel anxious, you can't sleep and so you drink too much coffee and end up a jittery mess. Suddenly problems that would rate a three on a difficulty scale feel huge and impossible. Of course they do! You are exhausted!

"I wake up every morning at 4 AM and sit there for at least half an hour thinking of all the things I have to do that day," a client shared with me. "Part of me really, really wants to go back to sleep, but sometimes I just give up and get up."

Don't give up and get up. There's a better way.

Make it Happen (45 Minutes)

So how can you take the lid off the pressure cooker of your life?

1. **Pray**

God knows what you are going through right at this moment. He is walking alongside you and ready to give you the help you need. When those feelings creep in, rebuke the enemy and ask God to take this burden from you. Remember Jesus said, "My yoke is easy and my burden is light" (Matthew 11:30).

The wonderful thing is that God's door is always open. You can pray any time, day or night. And, for a profound experience, pray together with your husband. Stop for a moment. Hold each other's hands and pray over this stressful situation. Here's one from my heart to yours:

Dear sweet Lord, you know the troubles that are plaguing our beautiful marriage. The pressure has become too much, God. It's too much for us to bear without you. I ask you to come alongside us and lift us up out of this darkness and into your light. I thank you for restoring our hope. I thank you for taking our burdens from us. We give you these ashes and you will trade them for beauty. You can do anything, God. We are amazed by you. In Jesus' name, Amen.

2. **Talk About It**

I can't tell you how many people we have coached that share their pain and their spouse is shocked (like mine was!). If you aren't sleeping because of your workload, talk about it! If you feel like you need to drink a bottle of wine to quell the anxiety, talk about it! If you are so angry you could spit, talk about it! You are not weak because you have needs. You are strong for admitting them.

If you know that things aren't right in your spirit but can't yet verbalize the cause, I encourage you to start a journal. There's something about a beautiful book with clean white pages that allows you to break down the walls of your heart. Go get yourself one with a cover that speaks to you. You know, that one with the Victorian garden overflowing with soft pink hydrangeas, or the one with the bold black polka dots on a white background. Get one that is so YOU. Let the words spill out and the truth will emerge.

3. **Action Plan**

Invite the Holy Spirit in and you will be guided as you plan. Your workload *can* be redistributed. Priorities *can* be shifted. Timing *can* be changed. Address the root of the problem and plan outward.

In our case, money was the main stressor. We worked together to find a new source of revenue that would be more reliable. It didn't fix things overnight but knowing that we were rowing in the same direction reminded me that I have a teammate in this journey. You do too. Talk through until you can feel the pressure leaving your body. That will tell you that you are on to something. Pray through, friend.

A quick note: Shortly after our money planning session, my husband asked me to dance in the middle of cooking dinner. He said, "I think we are happier than we have ever been." I laughed because I felt like we were more stressed than we'd ever been. He began to sing Kenny Loggins is his off-key voice, "And even though we ain't got money, I'm so in love with you, honey. Everything will bring a chain of love, love. And in the morning when I rise, you bring a tear of joy to my eyes and tell me, everything's gonna be alright..."

Everything is going to be alright. I promise.

ANALYSIS PARALYSIS

Having a plan is one thing. Executing it is another. Once you've spilled out your heart, you expect action. But that isn't always the outcome. We get trapped in the *how* and the *why* and the *when* and we can get stuck in that spin cycle for months or even years.

Wikipedia defines *analysis paralysis* as "the state of over-analyzing (or over-thinking) a situation so that a decision or action is never taken, in effect paralyzing the outcome."

We see this issue most often with couples that are in the midst of making a big decision. One of them is ready to go and the other is doing everything but making the actual decision. They are terrified about making the "right" choice and think that they will find the answer if they just get a little bit more information. They do end up making better-informed decisions in the end, but the cost is high, and of course there is never a risk-free path.

Gretchen Rubin of The Happiness Project describes it this way: "Satisfiers make a decision once their criteria are met; when they find the hotel or the pasta sauce that has the qualities they want, they're satisfied." In contrast, "Maximizers want to make the best possible decision; even if they see a bicycle that meets their requirements, they can't make a decision until they've examined every option."

If you are a maximizer and your husband is a satisfier, your agendas are completely different. You want to get it right; he just wants to get it done. Your intentions are sound and noble. You don't want to be the one to mess this thing up for your family and your employees. And yet, you can easily enter into decision fatigue.

We make thousands of decisions a day and our brains have a certain capacity to make those decisions. We choose what to eat for lunch, determine how much to budget for that project, and figure out who is going to pick up the kids from baseball. When we are lingering (and sometimes obsessing!) over a decision, our brains use an inordinate amount of energy on that task and we are left with little energy to tackle all the rest of life's demands. The result? We make poorer decisions about everything else. We watch TV instead of talking to our spouses or playing with our kids. We eat unhealthy foods and ignore exercise because we're just too tired. Meanwhile, our spouses are getting the short end of the stick.

"It's time to expand, Jim. You know it is," said our client, Sonia. Her arms were crossed and challenge was in her eyes.

"I agree! Why do you think I've been looking into the best direction to take?" he added defensively. He rested his elbows on the conference table and dropped his face in his hands. It was obvious that this conversation had been brewing for quite a while.

"Yeah, for six months," she replied under her breath.

This couple was trapped in a battle of wills.

We explored the impact this was having on their relationship and discovered that this expansion was the topic of virtually every conversation at home. Jim's mind wandered during dinner when his kids told him about their day. He spent hours each night researching the expansion and his wife felt ignored and very irritated. She had recommended the path they should take nearly five months before. She felt as if he didn't trust her judgement. He was overcome with anxiety and fear.

Swarthmore College conducted four separate studies that showed the negative psychological effects of being a maximizer.

1. Maximizers reported significantly less life satisfaction, happiness, optimism, and self-esteem, and significantly more regret and depression, than satisfiers.

2. Maximizers were more likely to engage in social comparison and counterfactual thinking (e.g., *What if I had chosen option number 2 instead?)* and experienced more regret and less happiness after making a consumer decision.

3. Maximizers experienced a greater increase in negative mood when they did not perform as well as their peers.

I did some research to uncover what God has to say about decision-making. Here are just a few notes from the NIV version of the Bible:

"Trust in the Lord with all your heart, and do not lean on your own understanding. In all your ways acknowledge him, and he will make straight your paths" (Proverbs 3:5-6).

"Do not be anxious about anything, but in everything by prayer and supplication with thanksgiving let your requests be made known to God. And the peace of God, which surpasses all understanding, will guard your hearts and your minds in Christ Jesus" (Philippians 4:6-7).

"And your ears shall hear a word behind you, saying, 'This is the way, walk in it,' when you turn to the right or when you turn to the left" (Isaiah 30:21).

The Bible is very clear on this one. We are to give our decisions to God, let go of our anxieties, and spend time listening intently for what direction *He* wants us to take. It's not easy. But there's a reason "fear not" appears 365 times in the Bible. He gives us one verse for every day.

I needed help giving something to God once (or maybe 1,000 times!) and I sought advice from an 80-something elder of my church. He asked me how often I pray to surrender my concern. "Every morning," I said proudly.

"There are times I have to do it every minute, Kate. I give it to Him and then I snatch it right back. Nobody ever said that one time would do it. You have to be persistent."

The answer does not lie in persistent research but in persistent prayer. Give it up to God as many times as it takes. It may take 1,000 times. It may take 100,000 times. But don't give up. I know it feels easier to be in control but our God is sovereign and His will always prevails. His timing is perfect. Keep working like it depends on you and praying like it depends on God.

Make it Happen (30 Minutes)

Is analysis paralysis invading your marriage in some way? Let's eradicate it.

1. **Air the Dirty Laundry.**

   Open up about any circular conversations you have been having that have delayed forward movement. Express your frustrations but also acknowledge his. Is he overwhelmed? Are you feeling undermined because he won't respond to your suggestions? Tell each other in a loving way. Hold each other's hands (do it even if you don't feel like it. There's great power in touch.). Repeat back what you heard him say and have him do the same for you. "It sounds like you are just so overwhelmed with the acquisition that you can't even think straight. Do I have it right?" The simple act of mirroring lets him know you aren't on opposite sides anymore. Sometimes showing can help telling: move to stand beside him, arms touching, and with your outside arm, point to a spot out in front of you both. "We're not on opposite sides," you can say. "We are next to each other, looking out there at this issue together. Facing the problem together means we'll resolve it together."

2. **Let Go and Let God.**

   Each time the worry monster creeps into your head, ask God to show you the way and "be a lamp to your feet and a light to your path" and then let it go. Do it every day, every hour, or every minute if you have to. Keep working and knowing that God is doing the same. He's got this!

3. **Agree on Must-Haves and Set a Drop-Dead Date.**

   For example, if you are ready to buy a new home but have already looked at 50 houses, it's time to call the game. Something is missing. Sit down and list out the top three must-haves (more if you can agree). Let's say you want the house to be on two acres of land, cost under $500K, and be within five miles of the kids' school. List out the properties that fit those criteria and set a date for a decision.

Early in the process, it is sometimes helpful to each list your own "criteria for rejection." Often we know what we don't want sooner than we can pinpoint our must-haves. This can be a real learning experience, by the way. Did you know that he would reject any house that had a garage door facing the street? Now you can save a lot of time in your searches.

You may decide to forgo home-buying at this time, but it must be a joint decision. Once the decision is made, curb your curiosity. Put down realtor.com. You can do it.

"Just make the best decision you can with the information you have," my mom always says.

Great advice.

It's important to take time to write down what you've agreed on:

We will decide on (insert pending decision)
________________ by (drop dead date)
________________ as long as the following criteria are met:

-
-
-

Now kiss on it.

SEEING AND SEEKING ABUNDANCE

"In your presence, there is abundant joy." Psalm 16:11

It takes work to stop believing the world's message that shines everywhere in neon lights: "MORE IS BETTER!!!" We think we want to have it all. We want the beautiful home, the latest car, private schools for the children, and the ability to "add to our cart" whenever we want it. The world tells us that things and money equals success and happiness. The problem with this model is that it never seems to be enough for us to feel satisfied or complete. At least not for more than about five minutes.

Have you ever noticed what goes on sale at every Target and Walmart on January 1st? Storage bins. They spend all of November and December telling you that you can't live without all these amazing things and all of January encouraging you to pack it away in $5 worth of plastic.

Our pastor's wife has a rule that she won't buy something if she can see herself selling it at a garage sale some day. Isn't that a great rule? The unfortunate thing is that I love garage sales. I love anything that costs $20 and under. I can fill a cart at T.J. Maxx and spend a hundred bucks without blinking an eye, but if I need to buy a $100 rug, I can't do it. My stomach clenches; I could get so much MORE with that money. (How do you think I know when those storage bins go on sale?)

J.D. Rockefeller was asked how much money would be enough. He answered, "Just a little bit more."

The problem with that mentality is that it can lead to a scarcity mindset. If you say, "We don't have enough time to spend with one another while building this business," or "There's no way we can afford to take vacations together in the start-up phase," then you're right. However, you can make another choice. You can see abundance all around you. You can visualize a team that is competent to execute your vision, so that you can spend more time together. You can imagine more than enough funds to get away once a year. You can be grateful for a date night at home thanks to Scrabble™ and a six-pack. You can be grateful for landing your first client, or for meeting payroll this month. "Leverage an abundance mentality and grateful attitude in your marriage, and you can expect your relationship to improve," says Daphne Mallory in the *Huffington Post*.

Dane and I experienced a difficult but character-building season, releasing ourselves from the chains of materialism. This is an excerpt from my blog that sheds light into that struggle.

I am so thankful that God doesn't give up until I understand what He is trying to tell me. He repeats himself over and over again until I get it, whether it's through music, a verse or just a conversation with a loving friend. Over the past few weeks, I have felt that He is reminding me to be aware of the abundance in my life. I read the verse, "In your presence, there is abundant joy" one morning and it jumped out at me. My husband used the word abundant later that day when describing the amount of clothes our children have in their closets. I heard a story on the radio a few days later about a food drive for kids that don't have enough to eat over the weekend and the DJ said, "Share your abundance with those that truly need it." So I started to pay attention.

We have already invested much of our year shaving our finances and ridding ourselves of the clutter in our home. This year had been about giving things up. It had been about sacrifices. Or was it? I watched my kids eat three different breakfasts over the course of one morning and felt thankful for the food in our home. I walked through our playroom and, instead of feeling annoyed about the toys strewn all over the floor,

I was aware of the abundance of toys my children had been given. We have more than we need of everything.

But abundance isn't just about stuff. It's about the gift of our relationships. I began to think about the incredible friendships I've been given this year. I thought about the growth I have seen in myself and in my marriage. I realized, once again, what a gift it is to stay home and teach my children every day (even on the crazy days!). And then this beautiful reverie was interrupted.

"We need to cut back a bit more," my husband said as he flipped the pork chop he was frying.

My head shot up from my phone. "What do you mean?" I asked, suddenly feeling defensive.

"Our spending is out of control," he said plainly. "It's not big stuff, but all the little stuff is adding up. It's not just you, babe. I'm a spender too. We probably should just go back to cash so we know our limits." He smiled turning to look at me. Instead of an agreeable wife, he found a dark storm.

"Our spending is not out of control! I barely spend any money ever!" I took a deep breath, knowing I was behaving like a spoiled child. "Let's just take a look at the account."

I pulled up our bank account on the computer and was stunned at the numbers staring back at me. Our spending had doubled over the last three months. I wish I could say I was contrite but I wasn't. I was angry. I felt that I had already given up so much. How could we cut back more without keeping my kids out of the activities they wanted, eliminating date nights, or getting rid of other things that helped us all maintain our sanity? I told my husband I needed to let all this sit for a while.

The next morning as I prayed I heard the quiet voice in my heart say, "abundance." Immediately I began to feel more peace. I realized that God had been preparing my heart for that conversation. He knows my weaknesses and wanted to remind me to stop focusing on the sacrifices and start seeing the gifts that He has blessed us with. We can still do all the free activities for kids. We can still have date nights under the stars with a bottle of wine. I haven't lost anything. The Lord's abundance never changes, no matter what my bank account says. And for that, I am thankful.

Make it Happen (15 Minutes)

There will be many times in this journey of life and business ownership that you will not have enough of something. Time and money are limited resources, or at least they often seem that way. But God's love and blessings have no limits. Our fulfillment will never come from stuff. (Sorry, T.J. Maxx.) Our fulfillment can only come from our Lord and savior.

I always imagine our lives as a big jigsaw puzzle. There are pieces that represent family and work and fun and God. If we try to squeeze cars or clothes or big trips into God's place, they will not fit. None of those things will bring you the same joy that knowing Him will give you.

Are you trying to squeeze other things into the God-shaped void? Are there things you are coveting? Join me in my journey to change that. As you walk through your day today, I want you to open your eyes to all you already have. Imagine yourself on a scavenger hunt seeking out God's blessings. Here are some clues to get you started:

Open your pantry and your refrigerator. Do you have enough food?

Take a peek in your closet. What do you see?

Do you have a car or reliable transportation to get you where you need to go?

Scan your office. Do you have the technology and supplies you need to do your job?

Talk to your children and your spouse. How do they bless you?

Take a walk outside. Smell the air, open your eyes to God's creation. Take a picture if it moves you.

Jesus doesn't promise abundant stuff, but He does promise abundant joy. If you find yourself slipping back into the old habit of wanting more, fall back on this wisdom from Philippians 4:8. "Whatever is true, whatever is noble, whatever is right, whatever is pure, whatever is lovely, whatever is admirable—if anything is excellent or praiseworthy—think about such things."

This I pray for you today.

GETTING REAL

Admitting weakness isn't easy, even with the people we love the most. There is so much pressure to provide, to be strong, to know what to do. Society pushes images on us that seem to shout, "Look! They have their life together! You should too!"

But 2 Corinthians 12:19 tells us, "My grace is sufficient for you, for my power is made perfect in weakness."

It feels counterintuitive to all the world teaches us. How can it be better to be weak? We want to believe that we've got this. We want to control our destiny and take charge of our future. Fully embracing this truth from the Lord means that we surrender all control. We trust His love fully and we fall on our knees saying, "I can't do this alone. I need you."

This cannot happen when you are too busy doing to get to the business of feeling. Burying your emotions feels noble at first. You are pressing on. You are getting things done—feelings can be handled later. You can't exactly have a meltdown in the middle of the conference room, right? But you do have to have that meltdown eventually.

Suppressing emotions causes you to withdraw or be half-present in all facets of your life. Your brain is processing those big feelings and it causes your mind to wander back to that place instead of staying in the moment. Sometimes I will be cooking dinner while mentally replaying a difficult conversation. I rewrite what he should have said, I beat myself up for what I said, and I either end up feeling guilty or justified. When my kids talk to me, I jump because I've become so immersed in my own thinking!

It may not seem like a big deal at first, but if you continue to distance yourself from those you love the most, the pain will grow and your relationships will suffer. When you are not present, you are taking yourself away from your loved ones. There is tremendous cost in not being present, and no benefit. Worrying about the future brings up fear;

worrying about the past leads to depression. You've seen this quote (attributed to Anonymous):

"Yesterday is history. Tomorrow's a mystery. Today is a gift. That's why it's called 'the Present'!"

When you are present, you can notice your feelings, i.e., your emotions as well as your body's physical cues. You can learn the signs for yourself. My friend shared that if she notices her temples are throbbing, she must figure out what she needs to apologize for and to whom—as soon as she takes that action, no more headache!

Like steam escaping a boiling teapot, your unexpressed emotions will scream out in inappropriate ways. You might start snapping at people for small mistakes, or break down in tears anytime there is a note of criticism in someone's voice. It won't seem rational and you'll ask yourself why you are so upset about such a tiny thing. If you aren't careful, you will minimize your feelings even further. After all, you're overreacting about so many things, right? Wrong. Your body is sending you a signal that it's time to turn off the burner on your boiling emotions.

"You don't want to end up under the desk," my mom said to me one day when I was sharing my frustration with the process of growing the business. She was referring to a time when the stress became so great and the pain so hidden that she just quit in the middle of the day. She hung up her phone, crawled into the cubby under her desk and cried for hours. When she finally emerged, it was clear that she needed professional guidance to get her out of this emotional darkness.

A study conducted by psychologists from *Harvard School of Public Health* and the *University of Rochester* found that suppressing emotions may increase the risk of dying from heart disease and certain forms of cancer. This confirms earlier studies that have linked negative emotions like anger, anxiety, and depression to the development of heart disease.

It makes sense; when you refuse to acknowledge strong emotions, your body is trapped in fight or flight mode. Stress is at its highest. When you make the conscious decision to become vulnerable, the stress hormones relax and begin to dissipate.

I sometimes imagine my negative emotions as little black fuzzy gremlins inside my brain and heart. They have these sour faces and they are throwing constant temper tantrums. They bounce around, wreaking havoc on my life perspective, my relationships, and my ability to focus. Even worse? They multiply quickly. The longer I leave them there, the bigger they grow. But the opposite happens once I begin to talk about them and pray about them. They weaken. They shrink. Eventually, they disappear.

Genesis 2:18 says, "It's not good for man to be alone; I'll make a helper suitable for him." God knew that we needed each other in this life. I have searched the Bible for references to independence and I haven't found a single one. There are, however, multiple verses about dependence on God. He knew that marriage would teach us what an interdependent relationship looks like and help us to understand that He will always be there for us.

Your husband can be that safe place for you and you can be that safe place for him. Sometimes getting real isn't easy because of the response you are expecting. Maybe he's dismissive. Maybe he teases you. Maybe he tries to fix it rather than hearing you out completely. Those concerns have to be addressed head on. It's alright to say, "I am going to share some things with you and I just need you to listen and then pray with me." We, as women, so often expect our husbands to know what we are thinking. Tell him what you want instead. If he doesn't follow through with that promise, you can remind him of the boundary during the conversation.

Our church went through a major upheaval when we lost our pastor and our associate pastor in the same week. One was planned, the other wasn't. My husband was the president of the church at the time and all the administrative decisions fell on his shoulders. He was traveling extensively for work and to say he was overwhelmed is an understatement. Now he was tasked with finding an interim and then permanent pastor.

He approached the ordeal with professionalism. He sought advice from churches in our diocese, posted on job boards, reached out to the community and formed a committee to manage this major decision. He researched his heart out to make sure he was doing the right thing. Six months passed and we had zero leads on a permanent pastor. Suddenly, his confident exterior began to crumble.

He was near tears one morning and I felt God urging me to meet him in prayer. He opened up about the toll this process was taking on him and I was astonished. My husband had been overcome by stress and this was the first time he had opened up about it. He said to me, "I have done everything by the book! I don't understand! I can't do this anymore!"

I heard God saying to my spirit that His power would blow us away. I wrapped my arms around Dane's waist and rested my head on his chest and prayed this prayer:

Lord, we thank you for this process. We know that you are preparing the perfect person for this position. I thank you for my husband and that you have trusted him with this enormous challenge. I ask that you show him your power, Lord. Bring us a pastor. Now. Today. He is tired and you tell us that your yoke is light. We trust that truth. We surrender to you, Lord. In Jesus' name, Amen.

Dane left for work that day and felt this urge to call a person that had left our church during the upheaval. "Hey, Dane! I've been meaning to call you! I've got a guy that might be a great candidate for First Christian."

That guy has been our pastor for three years. Because Dane got real with me that morning, I was able to reach toward him and lift him up to God. Because Dane got real with me, God answered that prayer with immediacy. Because Dane got real with me, I felt like I could be part of the solution and, therefore, his true partner.

Make it Happen (60 Minutes)

Set aside some time with a bottle of wine or a cold glass of lemonade. Take a long walk or just curl up on the couch in your pajamas. It doesn't matter how you do it. It just matters that you take some steps toward interdependence. Explore the areas that are causing tension in your home. If naming your emotions is new to you or your husband, you may want to make up a quick cheat sheet of feelings. List out words like frustrated, angry, disappointed, and overwhelmed. Then fill in the blank in your mind. I feel ____ when you ____. Your body will automatically tell you if it fits. Once you figure out what feels right, use it. The more you do it, the easier it becomes. Here are some questions to help get you going:

- Are there any feelings you hide from your spouse, even with the best of intentions?
- What business stresses are overwhelming?
- Do you have worries about your children?

- How is the stress interfering with your relationship?

Stress Issues

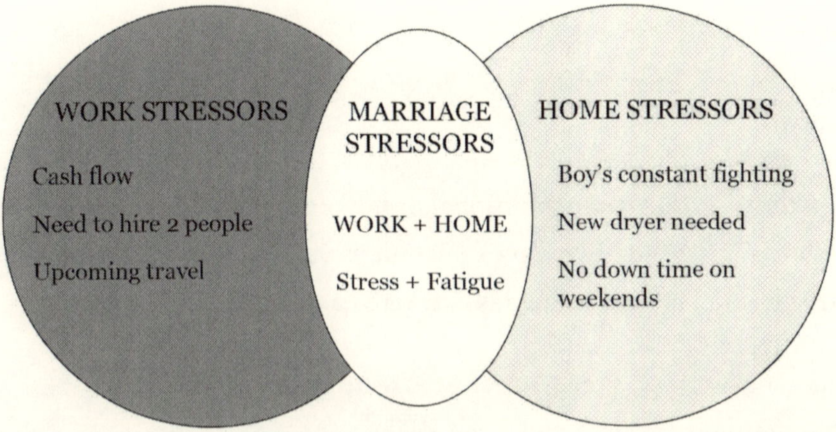

Diagram 2.0

Note: There is one key rule to this interaction. Stick with phrases that start with "I" rather than "You." No one feels loved when their shortcomings are being pointed out. Here's an example of both types of statements:

"You" statement: "You are constantly on your phone!"

"I" statement: "I feel ignored when you focus on your phone instead of me."

See the difference? They both bring up the issue of phone use but the second statement addresses the way you feel because of it. The "I" statement shows them your heart in a very real way. He can listen without defensiveness boiling up and overtaking your conversation.

- How can you help your husband feel more connected with you?

- How can he help you feel more connected with him?

You may realize through this that you need to talk to a Christian counselor. There is no shame in that! I've logged plenty of hours on a therapist's couch and each time I am changed for the better. Sometimes you just need to be understood and guided during difficult times. You can visit www.christiancounselordirectory.com for a list of therapists near you.

Whether you talk to a professional or not, keep this conversation going with your husband. Whenever something comes up that causes you pain, bring it up in a loving way. You deserve to be heard and so does he.

If getting along and reducing stress are not compelling enough reasons to express your feelings and respectfully communicate with one another, keep in mind that neglecting to do so is going to kill your business. It is your responsibility to keep your relationship "in good shape" so you both can hold up the walls of the business you are building. If either of you is too weak, serious problems can arise. The exercises I outline may seem simple, but don't skip them! Just like doing pull-ups can strengthen you in many different ways, working on your communication and God-centered relationship will prove absolutely necessary to successfully navigate the twists and turns a business is bound to take. Stay strong!

3

Repriortizing Your Life

You shall love the Lord your God
with all your heart and with all your soul
and with all your might.

Deuteronomy 6:5

The verse above is part of Jewish law that was well known at the time of Jesus' ministry. A teacher of the Old Testament challenges Jesus in Matthew 22 by asking him to reveal the greatest commandment. He is trying to trick Jesus. There is much debate about which laws to keep and which to disregard, and he wanted to pick a familiar argument. Jesus answers, "You shall love the Lord your God with all your heart and with all your soul and with all your might." He then adds, "And the second is like it. Love your neighbors as yourselves."

Jesus shows us so clearly that loving God isn't enough because it can become self-centered. If we are only focused on our own eternity, we can fall into the trap of self-righteousness and selfishness. We must also love others as we want to be loved.

The Bible clearly lists our priorities:

1. A relationship with Jesus Christ

   "I am the Alpha and the Omega, the First and the Last, the Beginning and the End," declares Jesus in Revelation 22:13.

2. Family

   "God decided in advance to adopt us into his own family by bringing us to himself through Jesus Christ. This is what he wanted to do, and it gave him great pleasure," in Ephesians 1:5 NLT.

3. Work

   God instructs you to subdue the earth and rule over his creation in Genesis 1:28.

Knowing your priorities and living your priorities are two very different things. Living your priorities means that you use them as a lens through which you make every decision. If an opportunity or choice interferes with your priorities, you do not do it. If a client wants to schedule a meeting that falls in the same time slot as your son's baseball game, you would suggest a different time because your family is higher on your priority list than your job.

Priorities

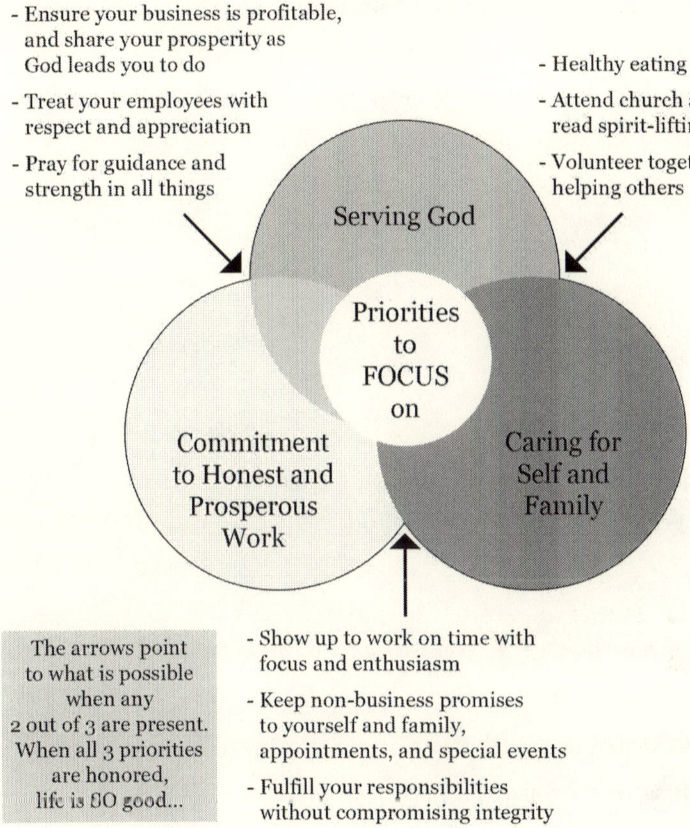

Diagram 3.0

Knowing your priorities is a good start; however, it simply means you understand what they should be and implement them "when you can." The squeaky wheel gets the grease, as they say. The phone rings in the middle of date night and you answer it. The softball team asks you to join and you say yes even though it means you miss family dinner four out of five weeknights. You start skipping your prayer time so that you can sleep in an extra half hour. None of those things are huge; in fact they are all small choices. But when you put them all together in a big picture, it's easy to see where priorities lie.

How do I know? Because I really messed this up for a while.

My husband and I had two small children at the time and we had lost touch. I was in survival mode. I was focused entirely on the needs of the kids and we had somehow begun to disconnect. Our relationship consisted of the business of marriage. Routine questions like "what time will you be home?" or "what do you want for dinner?" were the substance of our conversations.

That awesome God of ours always has perfect timing—our church announced an opportunity to attend a "FamilyLife Weekend to Remember" retreat. We said *yes* without hesitation (except for my constant worry that the baby would be okay without me) and headed to Lake Mary, Florida, a few weeks later. I left that weekend a changed woman.

FamilyLife shared the top three family priorities as "God, Spouse, and Children." This was hard for me. I saw my children as these tiny beings that demanded our love and attention at all times. If they interrupted, I felt compelled to explain to them that it's rude to interrupt before resuming my conversation (even if it's the 600th time I've told them). If they wanted to play, many times I would drop what I was doing to play. I realized that weekend that sometimes I ended up dropping my husband in the process.

He didn't say that to me, but, as I listened to the speaker listing a family's priorities, I suddenly saw how off-balance our own had become. When the speaker began talking about what marriage means to the children, he said simply, "You are their whole world. They will learn what it means to see love between a man and a woman by watching you interact with each other." It hit me that he was absolutely right. I flashed to all the times that I had asked my husband to wait to tell me all his stories about his day until after the kids went to bed. I remembered all the nights that I crashed by 9 PM without ever hearing them. And I decided that my priorities had to change.

I talked to my husband that night in our hotel room and we started to fall into an old pattern. "How about scheduling time to talk at eight, when the kids go to bed?" my husband suggested. Then we realized that the kids wouldn't see us making our marriage a priority if we did that. "I know, how about a walk every night after dinner? We can talk while the kids explore," he said. "Done," I said.

As we walked the halls of the conference, we came across a book called, *Moments with You*, by Dennis and Barbara Rainey. It gave us a passage a day to read together, then one question to talk about and a prayer to say together. I wasn't sure if he would go for it, but he was eager to try it. We decided to wake up at 6:30 each morning and spend time reading that together. I figured that we could always find 15 minutes.

The 15 minutes we planned overflowed into a half hour. The boys would sometimes pile into our bed and witness us spending time together. Even more importantly, I learned new things about my husband I thought I knew inside and out. There's nothing better in the world.

I know you want to live your priorities. Let's talk about how to embrace the top three and create an authentic and fulfilling life.

SERVING GOD

"I am the Alpha and the Omega, the First and the Last, the Beginning and the End" (Revelation 22:13).

This scripture holds particular power in my heart because it marked the beginning of my parents' relationship. They worked at the same company and my dad wrote "Alpha" on her desk calendar after their first date. He said, "I knew it was the beginning of something incredible."

When we serve God and place Him at the front of our life, it is the beginning of something incredible. I did not grow up in church but I did have a Godmother that took her role seriously. She gave me devotionals, invited me to church, and bought me my first Bible. I read those each morning and felt content with my relationship with God. I compartmentalized my life and put God in a 30-minute block in the morning. But God wanted so much more from me—He wants more of you, too.

The past five years have shown me that God wants to be our best friend. He wants to be the shoulder we cry on, the place we go for advice, the source of strength and encouragement. As we lift our hands in worship or drop to our knees in prayer, He fills us with his Holy Spirit. He whispers the things we need to hear into our hearts and reveals truths when we surrender every aspect of our lives to Him.

I did an amazing Bible study called "Experiencing God" that helped me deepen my connection with our Lord. It explained that he speaks to us through scripture (it literally jumps off the page when He wants you to see His truth!), through other Christians, and in everyday happenings if you are listening. But the only way we can develop that friendship is to spend time with Him. His greatest desire is a relationship with you. That relationship grows through worship, prayer, study, and servanthood. It completes you.

I watched a documentary on the worship band, Hillsong, and Joel Houston shared some beautiful imagery. He explained that he sees the cross as a reflection of our relationship with Jesus. The long part is worship. We reach up, surrender our lives and ask God's love and blessings to fill us completely. Once we are full, we stretch out our arms to share Jesus' love with the world.

There are seasons when you will need to be filled and seasons when you are ready to stretch out your arms and serve. But don't ever forget the second part. The cross isn't a cross without both components. I love how the story of the servants in Luke illustrates how God feels about this. Take a minute to read and meditate on this scripture:

> *"While the people were listening to these things, Jesus proceeded to tell a parable, because he was near to Jerusalem, and because they thought that the kingdom of God was going to appear immediately. Therefore he said, "A nobleman went to a distant country to receive for himself a kingdom and then return. And he summoned ten of his slaves, gave them ten minas, and said to them, 'Do business with these until I come back.' But his citizens hated him and sent a delegation after him, saying, 'We do not want this man to be king over us!' When he returned after receiving the kingdom, he summoned these slaves to whom he had given the money. He wanted to know how much they had earned by trading.*
>
> *"So the first one came before him and said, 'Sir, your mina has made ten minas more.' And the king said to him, 'Well done, good slave! Because you have been faithful in a very small matter, you will have authority over ten cities.' Then the second one came and said, 'Sir, your mina has made five minas.' So the king said to him, 'And you are to be over five cities.' Then another slave came and said, 'Sir, here is your mina that I put away for safekeeping in a piece of cloth. For I was afraid of you, because you are a*

severe man. You withdraw what you did not deposit and reap what you did not sow.' The king said to him, 'I will judge you by your own words, you wicked slave! So you knew, did you, that I was a severe man, withdrawing what I did not deposit and reaping what I did not sow? Why then didn't you put my money in the bank, so that when I returned I could have collected it with interest?' And he said to his attendants, 'Take the mina from him, and give it to the one who has ten.' But they said to him, 'Sir, he has ten minas already!' 'I tell you that everyone who has will be given more, but from the one who does not have, even what he has will be taken away." Luke 19:11-26

The Lord gives you gifts, passions, and talents. He expects you to use them for His glory, just as this king expected interest. Business acumen can be used to help young entrepreneurs succeed. A passion for children can lead you to teaching a Sunday school class. He blesses you so that those blessings can overflow and rain down on his kingdom. He trusts you with more and more "authority" when you are "faithful in every matter." And yet we are pulled in a million directions and feel like we can do His work later. We tell ourselves we will help out when "we have more time." Sometimes it takes someone we love kicking us in the rear to remember that there's no time like the present.

"I'd really like you to bring the kids to the Challenger baseball game," my husband said. He was volunteering for Sertoma, a service organization, to push the wheelchair of a man with disabilities around the bases. He constantly finds opportunities to serve. It's one of the things that made me fall in love with him, but it is overwhelming at times.

I looked at him, trying to find a nice way to say, "Are you kidding me? Have you seen our schedule for the weekend? Did you notice that the house is a disaster and this is my only day to get ready for the week?" Instead, I chose a more diplomatic track. "Let's play it by ear."

I saw the look of disappointment cross his face and felt the guilt creeping into my heart. He tried one more time. "It's just that I'd love for the kids to see these people with special needs playing baseball. I think it would really make an impact on them, you know?"

Great. Just great. How could I argue with that? "Okay, you're right. We'll go."

Time got away from me and as I scrubbed the bathroom sink I heard my husband saying it was time to go. I had him go in a separate car while I scrambled to get the kids ready and out the door. As we drove, I worried that the kids would say something that would be inappropriate or hurtful, as they had never been exposed to a large group of people with disabilities. "Hey guys? Just a heads up that the people playing might look different or talk differently than you do. Some may be in wheelchairs or use something to help them walk. But God designed each of them perfectly. Please make sure you don't point out their differences. I'm sure that would hurt your feelings if someone did that to you."

"I think it's so cool that they can play baseball in a wheelchair. That would be so fun!" my five-year-old said.

With that one comment, my perspective began to shift. I prayed that God would help my children and me to see the players' abilities, not disabilities. I prayed that I would be shown their gifts, their light, their joy. And He truly did.

I have never in my life seen so much enthusiasm in a game. They played with heart and dedication. They celebrated each other's victories and gave encouragement when there was a swing and a miss. One little boy smiled bigger than I've ever seen a child smile as he was pushed around the bases. "He just loves to run," his mom confided in me.

My five-year-old loved watching as well. "Did you see how far he hit that ball?! I hope I'm that good some day!" (I hope he's as kind and giving as his Daddy is someday, too.)

Serving isn't always convenient. In fact, most of the time it isn't. It interrupts your plans for your day or your week. But our time isn't really ours. We are here to do God's work. When we do, our souls are filled. We are amazed by grace in face of adversity, uplifted by faith and given a glimpse into what it means to truly love someone else more than we love ourselves.

There is great wisdom in Winston Churchill's words. "We make a living by what we get, but we make a life by what we give."

Make it Happen (15 Minutes)

What do you have that you can offer the world? Stop and take a moment to list out your passions, your blessings, your gifts. Ask God to bring you opportunities to let those blessings overflow into the lives of others.

Make a decision today to put God first. Spend time with Him every day. He follows you around all day so there isn't a time that's inconvenient. Sing worship songs to Him in the car. Take a quiet walk and listen for His voice. Stay up late reading scripture and talk to Him when the rest of the house is asleep. He is ALWAYS awake, waiting to listen. Give your decisions, your talents, your life to Him.

This is my prayer for you:

Dear sweet Lord, I thank you for the reminder that you are the Alpha and Omega. A real relationship with you is the beginning of something incredible. We are on a journey to learn how to see life through your eyes and walk through life with your heart. Help us, Jesus. Help us to lift our hands to you in worship and then spread our arms out to give your love to the world. Help us learn how to live like you. Help us love our spouses, children, friends, family and strangers like you would. Give us your grace, your love and your forgiveness as we grow. Be a lamp to our feet and a light to our path. We surrender, Lord. We love you, always and forever. In Jesus' name, Amen.

SERVING YOUR MARRIAGE

"Two are better than one because they have a good return for their labor. For if either of them falls, the one will lift up his companion" (Ecclesiastes 4:9-10).

You know that feeling you have when you get home after a long day? I just want to quiet my mind, pour a glass of wine, maybe cook something delicious or curl up on the couch and talk. The last thing I want to do is field a million questions and give commentary on Lego creations, art projects, and gymnastics tricks simultaneously. My husband used to be abrupt with this influx of information. He would hug each of the kids but then send them upstairs without paying much attention to the things they showed him. He would simply seek me out so that we could swap stories about our day. I wanted him to give the kids all the attention they desired; he wanted them to respect his need for 20 minutes with me. This led to many conversations about better ways to handle "re-entry," the transition time from work to home.

I understood why he wanted it but, to be honest, I spend so much time tuned in to my kids' needs that I can forget to think about his. I decided to try a different tactic this time. We told the kids that the first half hour was Daddy and Mommy time—after that, it was family time. It took months for it to actually sink in that we are serious about this time but it has completely changed our family dynamic. Dane and I cook together while we sip a glass of wine, or I just sit down and watch him do the work and feel grateful for a husband that cooks. We have time to tell funny stories, talk through big things that happened that day, or just sit in companionable silence. It reconnects us and after that 30 minutes, he's completely ready to step back into being an amazing dad.

Our three-year-old, Rosie, had taken a really long nap one day recently and she woke up in the middle of dinner. She curled up on the couch, still fuzzy from sleep. The song "My Girl" came on and Dane pushed his chair out from the dinner table and walked over to his baby girl. He scooped her up off the couch and held her tightly as he swayed to the music. He smiled a smile that is reserved only for her and asked her if he could dance with her to this song at her wedding. "Sure, Daddy. Sure, you can," she said as she laid her head on his shoulder.

We can't give when we are completely spent. We can't be expected to run on fumes. And yet, so often, we keep pushing ourselves and giving into everyone's demands. We say yes because we "should" and end up only being able to give half of what we normally could. The flight attendant always tells you, "Put your own oxygen mask on first before attempting to help another..." My husband reminded me that it's so much smarter to stop, refuel and then attend to the needs of those you love.

Make it Happen (15 Minutes)

Are you and your spouse tuned in to having personal and relationship needs met? Life can be so noisy and distracting and difficult. We tend to want our spouse to be the one thing we don't have to worry about. We focus on work and kids and team practices and homework and appointments. But where is the joy in that life?

It's time to reclaim the joy in your marriage. Don't worry—this isn't going to be some arduous thing you don't have time to do. This is a trip down memory lane. I want you to remember some very real details about falling in love.

How did he look at you? Was there mischief in his eyes or just complete and total devotion? Close your eyes and feel how you felt when he looked at you like that.

How did he touch you? Did he playfully tickle you or gently reach for your hand in moments when you least expected it? Feel that touch again.

What did he smell like? Maybe there was a certain cologne he wore, or maybe he used to work on cars and had a faint tinge of motor oil all the time. Can you smell it?

Where did you go? Were there places you experienced together or roads you drove down at twilight that light up your soul when you think about them? Be in that place for a moment.

This, my friend, is the person you are partnering with in service to God, your family, and others. This is the person that made your heart soar and your fingers tingle at the thought of touching them. Use all your senses to remember the earliest of times until you can just FEEL it; when you become immersed, you may even need some tissues as your emotions overflow. If you aren't even close to this, take a little more time to bring your memories more vividly to mind. Pictures, scrapbooks and songs will sometimes trigger those old feelings. Take all the time you need to bring your heart back to the very beginning of your love.

Your love has grown since then. It is broken in like a comfortable pair of jeans. You know the sounds he makes when he sleeps. You know every curve of his body. You know what he is going to say before he says it. That can seem boring or it can reflect the true intimacy you share. You choose the lens through which you view the world. Let's choose to see this as a beautiful foundation on which you can bring the spark, the fun, and the light back into your marriage. It's time to put a brand new shirt on with those old jeans.

Steal a flirtatious glance, tell an inside joke, slap his butt when no one is looking. Make time to talk—really talk. Go back to the places you used to go and reminisce. Hug and kiss. A lot. And pray together every day. It takes effort but it's amazing how little tiny flirtations and kindnesses create a stronger marriage.

There are mornings when I still have my hair in a towel and the kids are running around the house chasing the dog screaming with glee and Dane will say, "Alright, I've got to go. Let's pray."

The moment seems completely inopportune. The chaos is palpable. And yet when we join hands or I rest my head against his chest, all the noise falls away. We take turns leading prayer and his prayers remind me that he's been listening all along to the things I have shared with him. He may something simple like, "Thank you God for my beautiful wife. Help her to stop being so hard on herself. She's such an amazing person."

Those words have more weight when he brings them to our Father.

When we release our hands and open our eyes, the world looks different. We no longer feel the weight of the world on our shoulders. We have left the chaos for a few short minutes and entered into calm. We have connected with God and each other.

You both deserve to be put before everything but God. You both deserve to be loved completely and fully. It starts with you. Michael Jackson put it best in "Man in the Mirror".

He says that the change starts with you, the man in the mirror. It's up to you to make it right. Go make it right.

SERVING YOUR FAMILY

I received an invitation to a birthday party for a close friend and it said: "The best present is your presence." I stopped for a moment to let that sink into my heart. I love giving gifts and it seemed a slight to show up at a birthday party without a little something that reflected my love. And then God put this praise song in my heart. A dear friend sings it at our church and I could see her eyes closed and hands raised as she invited the Holy Spirit's presence.

> *"There's nothing worth more*
> *That will ever come close*
> *No thing can compare*
>
> *You're our living hope.*
> *In Your presence, Lord.*
>
> *Holy Spirit you are welcome here*
> *Come flood this place and fill the atmosphere.*
> *Your glory God is what our hearts long for*
> *To be overcome by your presence, Lord."*

I realized in that moment the power of presence. It means giving someone everything you are without distractions. It means inviting them to be everything they are without judgment and embracing them in that moment. No thing can compare to that kind of presence.

And yet, we let days and weeks and months pass without engaging with the people we love the most. We are at the dinner table but our minds are somewhere else. We're thinking about that email we need to draft or that difficult client that's been draining every ounce of our patience. We're thinking about going to the grocery store tomorrow and how to fit that in between baseball practice and haircuts. Our minds are perpetually focused on what's next rather than what's now.

"The ability to be in the present moment is a major component of mental wellness."

—Abraham Maslow

Jesus' disciples fought with this same thing during the last supper. They were so distracted by the impending events that they were not mentally present. "Interestingly enough, it's the one whom Jesus loved the most, John, who exhibits the most 'presence' with Christ," said Tim Popadic, Director of the Relationship Enrichment Collaborative. "In John 13:23, Scripture says, 'the one Jesus loved dearly, was reclining against Jesus, his head on his shoulder.' We get this visual of John's head against Jesus' shoulder, close enough to hear his heartbeat. In this act, John demonstrates to us the importance of slowing down, leaning in, and not letting any circumstance or moment pass without practicing the discipline of being present."

I don't know about you, but I certainly hope I can be more like John. I want to lean in to my loved ones. I want to hear their heartbeat and know what trials and triumphs they hold. My husband set a beautiful example of leaning in when our household was assaulted by illness.

I was sick twice in one week. Twice. The first time I was throwing up. The second time I had a cold. Meanwhile, my husband got the stomach thing and my oldest got the cold and we were all a hot mess. But there were blessings amidst all the tissues.

"I'll be home at lunch, babe," he said as he rubbed my back, looking worried.

"I'll be okay. I'll just put on a movie for the kids," I said as I ran to the bathroom to throw up my Gatorade breakfast. I wanted to believe that I would be fine. *I'm a mom. I'm tough. I've got this.* Except I didn't have it at all.

The barrage of requests from my 7, 5 and 2-year-olds was overwhelming. They were hungry and the sight of food was repulsive. They wanted to chase each other and movement made me nauseous to watch. I finally turned on a movie, hoping for stillness. Our lab puppy, Charlie, wanted none of it. He worked his way through the living room chewing up markers, the couch, the rug, and any toys that didn't belong to him. Each time, I would need to get up, redirect him, and give him one of his toys.

I lay back down, closed my eyes, and suddenly felt a poke in the eye. "Wake up, Mommy!" My littlest angel yelled. "No sweep! Great movie, Mommy. You wake up!"

"Honey, Mommy is tired and sick. I need to close my eyes. You enjoy the movie, baby girl."

Tears flowed. "No sweep, Mommy! It scary! Hold me up?"

I gave up and texted my mom an SOS. I asked her to come after lunch when my husband went back to work and she quickly agreed.

My husband arrived home with soup, crackers, and movies. I fell into his chest for a hug, grabbed my loot, and headed for the bedroom to sleep.

When I woke up three hours later, I found him sitting on the lanai next to a pool full of our kids and neighbor kids. I observed from the living room for a few minutes as he watched the kids' "cool tricks," applauded their big splashes and grabbed a wayward water wing out of the puppy's mouth. He seemed to balance it all seamlessly and I was overwhelmed with gratitude. I opened the door. "Hey, babe! I thought Mom was coming so that you could get back to work?"

"I told her to go home. I wanted to take care of you." It's no wonder I love this man.

A few days later, my oldest son said to my husband, "Daddy, I love that you are the kind of Daddy that stays with us when Mommy is sick. Instead of going back to work, you took care of all of us. I love that." My husband and I looked at each other and smiled. He had not only given me everything I needed and more, he had taught our son an invaluable lesson. I hope it's one that he never forgets.

Make it Happen (5 Minutes)

You can give your family the gift of your presence, too. Here are a few ideas to help you.

- Clear your mind

  If you're heading home from work, take the long way and unwind. It's tempting to stay on the phone and use that time to tie up loose ends but you will get home with your head still on that call. Let your mind wander wherever it needs to go. My mom calls this "wool gathering" and I think it's fitting. You are finding all the loose bits and gathering them into a big ball of thoughts. Some need your attention but most will just be fleeting glimpses of your day. Enjoy this time by yourself.

- Have an attitude of thankfulness

    Before you go into the house, say a prayer of thankfulness. Thank God for your family, for the blessing of time with them. Thank Him for giving you the opportunity to show them your love by being fully present. He will guide you back when your focus wavers.

- Disconnect

    Put the phone on the charger and keep the laptop in your bag. Even a glance at an email can send your brain spinning into problem-solving mode. This time is for your family. They only get a few hours a day with you. Lean in.

- Say yes when they need you

    Sometimes your life falls into a predictable schedule but many times it does not. One of the kids gets sick and needs to be picked up at school; your friend has a horrible day and really needs someone to talk to; your daughter needs help with homework when you planned on taking a hot bath. Embrace those times as a chance to give a gift. Yes, they are inconvenient but they are also beautiful expressions of Jesus' love.

SERVING YOUR BUSINESS

Owning a business isn't just a way to make money. It becomes this whole separate entity that you care for and nurture. You spend hours, months and years watching it grow or suffer, and you push hard to help it succeed. You've put your heart and soul into building this thing. It deserves your focus and dedication.

Growing up in a family business showed me how easy it is to get distracted.

"Can I talk to you?" my sister would say, peeking into my office. Before I could answer or even finish typing the sentence in my email, she was sitting on the couch talking through a fight she had had with a friend.

I would drop everything, grab us each a cup of coffee and sit on the couch until she felt heard and ready to get back to work. Sometimes we would decide to go out for a long lunch or get a pedicure because we "needed a break" and not return for two hours. Apparently we are not alone in this misuse of time.

By studying thousands of people, David Rock, co-founder of the NeuroLeadership Institute and author of *Your Brain at Work,* found that we are truly focused for an average of only six hours per week. Not per day. Per week! "You want to be really diligent with what you put into those hours," he writes.

Have you seen the movie, *Up*? There is a sweet and dopey dog that can rarely finish a sentence without exclaiming, "Squirrel!" and running in another direction. I believe our workplaces have become infested with "squirrels," meaning one distraction after another. We try to write a proposal and a Facebook notification comes up on our computer screen and our phone…squirrel!

We are working on budget projections and a text message notification pings...squirrel!

We are in the middle of a strategic planning meeting and our watch pings with an email. We check out for just a second to preview it…squirrel!

We believe that this is somehow making us more efficient. We are multitasking, after all. Research has proved the opposite is true. "It reduces our intelligence, literally dropping our IQ," says Rock. "We make mistakes, miss subtle cues, fly off the handle when we shouldn't, or spell things wrong." And remember, it is literally impossible to do two things at the same time. In the best case, you can get good at switching quickly back and forth, wasting energy, time, and lessening your effectiveness on each task.

Your business is too important for that nonsense.

Make it Happen (10 Minutes)

Here are a few tips to get you going.

1. **Hard Stuff First**

I love checklists. I have a whole system where I make my list and put a circle next to something that has been started and a check mark next to things that have been completed. I have a running list and add new things each morning then peruse the list to decide what to do first. Guess what I pick? The easiest one. Sometimes I even have to rewrite my list because there is something four pages back that I've been avoiding. Guess what research shows me? That's the worst thing to do.

"Alertness and memory, the ability to think clearly and to learn, can vary by between 15 and 30 percent over the course of a day. Most of us are sharpest some two-and-a-half to four hours after waking," writes Jennifer Ackerman in *Sex Sleep Eat Drink Dream: A Day in the Life of Your Body.*

That means the morning is the critical time to tackle creative projects, difficult problems and long-term planning. Your brain is rested and ready to go. It's fine to check a few of the easy things off the list first—I know that gives me an emotional boost when I'm able to accomplish something quickly. But don't avoid the hard stuff. Use the time when you are at your best to go after it. Completing what had been daunting provides great energy for tackling everything else.

2. **Schedule Tech Checks**

Larry Rosen, Ph.D., research psychologist and author of *iDisorder: Understanding Our Obsession With Technology and Overcoming its Hold on Us*, writes that we rarely "focus and attend" to any task for more than three to five minutes before getting distracted—primarily by emails, texts, and social media.

That's embarrassing to me. Five minutes is our max? I expect more out of my kindergartner! And yet, I feel that same pull to check if anything is happening that I need to take care of. It's like this invisible world of action that I must be a part of all the time.

I have learned over time that scheduling is the only way to get it done. I turn off the notifications that pop-up on my laptop, turn my phone upside down and on silent and then create an auto-response on my email. "I check email every 30 minutes and will get back to you then!" At first, this was painful. I wanted to be super responsive! I wanted to blow them away with my work ethic! Did I look like a lazy bum by doing this?

The opposite occurred. I realized that I'm not in a life or death business. There is never something that can't wait 30 minutes. Never. Even better? It's often resolved by the time I check it. When people don't get an immediate answer from me, they often seek another avenue of solving the problem. They reach out to someone else or look up the answer, or maybe calm down enough to gain some perspective on a difficult interaction. It's not your job to solve the problems of the world. Focus. They will be okay, I promise.

3. **Embrace Flexibility**

Every individual has a biorhythm or, "a cyclic pattern of physical, emotional, or mental activity said to occur in the life of a person." You've heard of *night owls* and *early birds*. You may not be either of those, but you certainly have a time that you work the most efficiently. The amazing thing about owning a business is that you can embrace your own rhythms and work when you are at your best.

Pay attention to your rhythms. Are you flying through your to-do list all morning only to hit a wall at 11:30? Do you drag through the day and come alive when the sun goes down? I encourage you to map how you feel throughout the day for an entire week. Write down the moments when your creativity and energy is thriving and when it begins to wane. See if environment changes that rhythm or if it stays the same regardless. I work best in the quiet of the morning with a candle lit. My husband loves to work with music playing and ESPN on mute in his office. This would make me certifiably insane but it works for him. What works for you?

Patterns will emerge when you review your week. Note them and use that to your advantage. Schedule your day according to those emerging patterns and be amazed at how much you can do in a day.

Still feeling a bit fuzzy? Stephen Covey designed an effective tool for prioritizing in his book, *Seven Habits of Highly Effective People,* called the four quadrants.

- In Quadrant I (top left), he lists items that are **important** and **urgent**. They are items that must be dealt with immediately.

- In Quadrant II, there are items that take focus and are necessary for the completion of your long-term goals. These are **important** and **not urgent**.

- Quadrant III is filled with things that are **urgent** but **not important** (An email telling you that coffee is free at the local coffee shop until 2!).

- Quadrant IV includes items you want to try and avoid all together. They are **not urgent** and **not important**. They are the time suckers that seem so much more appealing than the work in front of you.

Covey's research found that "highly effective people" value their time by investing their efforts in "important, not urgent" activities (Quadrant II).

Here's a sample of each quadrant:

	Urgent	Not Urgent
Important	I (MANAGE) • Crisis • Medical emergencies • Pressing problems • Deadline-driven projects • Last-minute preparations for scheduled activities	II (FOCUS) • Preparation/planning • Prevention • Values clarification • Exercise • Relationship building • True recreation/relaxation
Important	Quadrant of Necessity	Quadrant of Quality & Personal Leadership
Not Important	III (AVOID) • Interruptions, some calls • Some mails & reports • Some meetings • Many "pressing" matters • Many popular activities	IV (AVOID) • Trivia, busywork • Junk mail • Some phone messages/email • Time wasters • Escape activities • Viewing mindless TV shows
Not Important	Quadrant of Deception	Quadrant of Waste

Keep this visible so that when distractions arise (as they always do!) you can turn to this as a decision-making tool. If that distraction meets the qualifications of Quadrant I as urgent, take care of it. If, however, a pile of junk mail crosses your desk, avoid it. You have much better things to do with your time!

Also notice that relaxation and relationship-building are marked as important. You need those things to maintain a balanced life. Be sure you are including those things in your planning so that you have all the focus you need once you begin your work day.

4
No-Work Zones

My people will live in peaceful dwelling places,
in secure homes, in undisturbed places of rest.

Isaiah 32:8

You've figured out what is precious to you as you worked to prioritize your life. How are you going to protect it?

A dairy farmer purchases a head of dairy cows. What does he do before they come to his farm? Build a fence. Secure the fence. Ensure that the cows will be protected and have everything they need within that fence. That's exactly what we are going to do over the course of the next two chapters. We are going to protect what is important to you by building clear and secure boundaries.

Many people confuse standards and boundaries. If you, for example, won't wear flip-flops without having had a recent pedicure, that is a standard. You may feel like it is simply unacceptable to have exposed, unkempt or unpolished toes. (I am one of those people!) Someone else may only feel that a pedicure is necessary for a fancy evening out. That is their standard. It does not affect anyone else if you wear nail polish or choose to go *au naturel*. Reflect on what you have standards about, especially noting when they seem to differ with other people close to you. If you recognize it as *your* standard, you can more easily refrain from hoisting it on the shoulders of someone else. You are welcome to insist on using distinctly-shaped wine glasses, one for red, one for white. But when you are at someone's home as their dinner guest, I hope you would not complain if only one type was available for any wine. They have their own standards, and some will be looser than yours and some will be stricter. It's none of your business.

A boundary, however, is yours to define, own, and enforce. Setting boundaries has more to do with how you are setting up your life and environment, how you define the rules for everyone who wants to play in your game. You can set a boundary by telling people that they may not smoke in your car. You aren't telling them that they can't smoke at all—you are simply saying that your car is a no-smoking zone. This rule helps you feel safe and at peace. (Notice where you don't feel safe or at peace in your life, today. Bingo! That is where a boundary is missing.)

Setting clear boundaries cuts off misunderstandings and prevents power struggles. They define where our responsibility stops and another person's responsibilities begin. "Unclear boundaries can be one reason we have very destructive and dysfunctional relationships. On the other hand, depression, codependency, anxiety, and many other conditions can improve by becoming aware of and enforcing our personal boundaries," writes Allison Bottke in *Setting Boundaries with Difficult People.*

Boundaries are critical if we want to guard our relationships and safeguard our own hearts. We understand physical boundaries. When we climb out onto the balcony of a 20-story building, we expect a railing. And yet our relationships do not always have railings.

A marriage without railings is possible, but is it safe?

Take yourself through this checklist to find out if boundaries are affecting your life and your marriage:

- Do you find yourself sucked into silly fights constantly?
- Do you feel like you are constantly giving without getting anything back?
- Do you spend a lot of time defending yourself and feeling like things aren't your fault?
- Do you often feel taken advantage of?
- Do you feel the need to save people or fix their problems for them?
- Do you wish you had a more peaceful life?

If you answered yes to any of these, it's time to set some boundaries. Your motives are pure. You want to help. You want to be a valuable asset to your family and your business—but it can't be at the cost of your own sanity.

I have a no-kid boundary between 6:00 AM and 7:30 AM. I get up every morning to pray, write, and get my day organized. I need that time to feel centered and for God to prepare my heart for all the challenges and opportunities of the day. My husband does a beautiful job of keeping the kids away during that time but I found that when he travels for business, my time unravels.

"I haven't had any time in the morning and I'm starting to lose it," I complained over the phone to my husband. "I hear 'Mommy' and I cringe!"

"Is there any reason you aren't telling them to leave you alone?" asked my ever-practical husband.

"I did, but they won't listen!"

"Sounds like you need to make them listen."

I hate it when he's right. It was completely in my hands and yet I had convinced myself that I was the victim in the situation. Once I sat them down and explained that I needed uninterrupted time, they respected it. If they did pop their head into my bedroom, a simple reminder like, "This is my time to pray," prompted a quick exit. You see, they weren't respecting the boundary because I hadn't set it. Once it was clearly communicated, they were ready to comply. It is important to note that I've found that using a "mean" or "stern" voice is not necessary, but using a firm, intentional voice does get the message across. Also, be willing to repeat your clear boundary several times until they get it, each time using a firm but not exasperated voice.

The same is true in all of your relationships. Your family, your employees, your church and your friends all need to know where the railings lie in your relationship.

"A person with strong boundaries understands that it's unreasonable to expect two people to accommodate each other 100% and fulfill every need the other has," Mark Manson explains in *The Guide to Strong Boundaries*. A person with strong boundaries understands that they may hurt someone's feelings sometimes, but ultimately they can't determine how other people feel. A person with strong boundaries understands that a healthy relationship is not controlling one another's emotions, but rather each partner supporting each other in their growth and path to self-actualization."

Let's build some railings.

NO-WORK ZONES

Our pastor told a story about a boy with a kite. He had gotten to the very end of the string and he felt as if the kite was touching the clouds. He thought to himself, *If I let it go, it will probably go to outer space!! So* he released the line and the kite dropped to the ground.

He closed his point by saying, "A kite won't fly without being tethered. Freedom also requires boundaries."

You have tremendous freedom as an entrepreneurial couple. You are not bound by PTO (paid time off) days—you can go on vacation at a moment's notice. You don't have to deal with upper management—you are the final decision maker. You are not stuck in one cubicle all day—you can work from any spot you choose. Anything is possible. Work and life are truly one and the same. There is no "Honey, I'm home!" moment if you are together all day long. If you're sautéing onions and a work question pops into your brain, you ask it. Your business partner is right there; why not take advantage of it?

Dane and I often will go from problem solving about a client to telling a cute story about the kids and then on to a theological question that one of us finds interesting. Everything is intertwined and it feels impossible to place a "hard stop" on work topics at home. But it's a slippery slope.

When is it good to *compartmentalize* and when is it best to *integrate*?

Be honest...where is your work pile at home? The dining room table? The kitchen bar? Have you dedicated an entire room of your home as an office? A study by Scott Schieman of the *University of Toronto* found that 50% of people bring their work home. That number is even higher for those that "hold professional jobs with more authority, decision-making latitude, pressure, and longer hours." I would say that you and I both fit into that category, wouldn't you?

Entrepreneurs feel the pull of work constantly. Our phones ping and we want to respond immediately. Sometimes I will even "see" the person in my head waiting anxiously for my reply. I don't want to let them down! I need them to know I'm on it! But if I choose to answer the call, my kids just see that I'm choosing my phone over them. Instead of jumping in the pool with them, we are checking our email. Instead of talking to our spouses, we are on our laptops. But these choices can have long-term effects.

I grew up with parents that had amazing entrepreneurial drive. They started, grew, and sold seven companies by the time I was 18 years old. I always remember the business being the primary topic at the dinner table or in the car, but things got much worse once cell phones and the internet made it super easy for my dad to work from anywhere.

I vividly recall many life-shaping experiences from my childhood, like when we left the cold of Ohio for a family vacation to Siesta Key Beach in Florida in 1996. I remember the year because I had been cast as "Maria" in the *Sound of Music* my senior year and brought the script to run lines during vacation. My parents had rented a 60's cinder block condo that was decorated with flamingos and white wicker furniture that creaked when you sat on it. We could walk down a narrow alley to gorgeous white sand beaches where my sister and I spent hours laying in the sun. She lathered on oil as I put the third application of SPF 60 on my pale white skin. We were teens, old enough to want to be independent, but young enough to still be seeking our parents' attention.

But during that entire "vacation," my dad was present in form only, never tuning in to his family or the beautiful surroundings anyone would call *relaxing*. Dad found a small wicker entry table to set up his laptop and Sprint card that would allow him to connect to the internet using his cellular network. His cell phone was charged and ready and he spent virtually all day every day at that seat. As I rehearsed my lines with my mom, he would shush me and ask me to go in another room. Even the death ray stare of my mom wouldn't deter him. He paced the tiny condo barking orders into his cell phone, trying to maintain control from 1,000 miles away.

I remember feeling an anger simmer to the surface on that trip. I couldn't understand why he had even bothered coming if his focus was entirely on the company back north. It wasn't the first time he had chosen the business over time with his family, and it wouldn't be the last.

I confronted him and asked him to put down the phone, shut down the computer, take a walk on the beach. He gave me the dad look that told me I was venturing into dangerous territory and refused to engage in the conversation. I felt defeated, disappointed and angry. Running the company was number one. That was made clear, at least to my 17-year-old mind.

My dad is now a gentle and kind 60-something that has Jesus in his heart. "I would have given anything to have had God while I ran all those companies," he said to me as I interviewed him for this book. "It would have changed everything. I never thought of anyone but myself. Faith taught me to be so much more compassionate, you know?" He took a sip of Constant Comment tea. He drinks it out of a plastic mug he got from the hospital when I was born. I have never seen him use a different mug—the sight of it gives me comfort. "You guys were close to mom and I guess I figured she would take care of you, and I would take care of the company. Her primary thing was the kids and the house and my primary thing was the business. She worked too, but I was always the one who had the responsibility to make things happen. It would be very different if I had to do it over again."

There is a book called *The Top 5 Regrets of the Dying* written by a hospice nurse named Bronnie Ware. She counseled people as they faced death and uncovered their deepest regrets. All of them said they wished they had worked less and spent more time with their family and friends. They could see clearly what mattered and wished they had time to rewrite their past to align with their values. The beauty of this lesson is that we can decide *today* to live our lives differently.

The Bible gives us this wisdom as well. "The world and its desires pass away, but whoever does the will of God lives forever" (1 John 2:17). This world will try to convince you that your success and achievements matter more than anything. It will tell you lies about the glittering and beautiful life you will have once you get on the cover of Inc. Magazine. You know in your heart that this is not the secret to fulfillment. Fulfillment can only come from the Lord. He is the one that wants to put you on the cover so that you can glorify Him. He wants you to love your spouse "as Christ loves the church." He wants you to raise your children up in "the way that they should go." You cannot do that if you are only focused on selfish desires. You *can* do that through His power and Holy Spirit.

Make it Happen (60 Minutes)

Carve out an hour or two alone to dig deep on this one. In what areas are you letting your work life infect your personal life? What are some areas that boundaries are already present and bring harmony to your home? Be still and open your heart to where God is leading you. This is not a time to let those negative statements to go on repeat in your head. This is time to let God show you what your life could look like with true, clear boundaries that align with your priorities. Write it down, draw a picture if you sketch. Remember, you started this journey of entrepreneurship for freedom. Own it.

Next I'd like you to sit down with your spouse to share your vision and listen to their ideas for life 2.0. There are a couple ground rules for this interaction.

1. Pray together before you begin. Here's one to get you started. *"Dear Lord, we thank you for the wisdom you have given us through your Holy Spirit. We thank you for the gift of our*

differences and the ability to work through them even when it's hard. We ask that you fill our hearts with openness, love and possibility. Show us what you want for our home life together and give us the strength to trust you to make it happen. In Jesus' mighty name we pray, Amen."

2. Remember this wisdom from Proverbs 15:1: "A soft answer turns away wrath, but a harsh word stirs up anger." Know that your spouse may not see "their faults" as clearly as you do. Sit on your hands when you start to feel the need to finger point. We're all guilty of crossing boundaries when they haven't yet been clearly defined. Focus on setting boundaries instead.

Still struggling with where to start? Here's a quick example from a couple that has worked together for 30 years:

"We have three no-work zones," she said. "The bedroom is number one. No laptops, no work conversations, no checking email on our phones in the bedroom. It needs to be a sacred place for our marriage only."

These boundaries protect the energy inside the bedroom so that it is conducive to the purpose of the room, i.e., relaxation, intimacy, rest.

"Second is the patio and pool. That should be a fun place."

I agree. Who wants to text an angry client when you're sipping a margarita poolside?

"Third is our Friday date night," she concluded. "When he brings up work I actually wave my hands back and forth so that he will stop! It works!"

There will be areas where your vision aligns and other areas that surprise you. Talk through them and merge your ideas. Once your list of ideas has been compiled, pray for God to make them happen. God can do so much more than we could ever imagine.

MAKING TIME FOR YOU

If I asked you to list five of your hobbies, could you do it?

There was a period of my life when my main hobby was sleep. I craved it, fantasized about it, and truly enjoyed it. Of course, I had two children under three—that might explain it. My life was a big ball of craziness. Mornings started with a string of "mamamamama's," "MOMMY!! Guess what!?" and whines from our dog to be taken out. All in the first 30 seconds of waking up. Once I got to my cup of coffee, I had usually completed more tasks and tended to more needs than I ever did in an entire day as a single girl.

I remember crying to my husband when my youngest was about six weeks old that I hadn't been able to find time to pee in five hours because someone needed fed, walked, put to bed, played with, etc. He gave me an incredulous look and said, "Why don't you just let them know they need to wait a minute so that you can go?" How could this have escaped me? It always seemed like their needs were much more urgent and important. I had made the decision to put my needs last. It was up to me to change it.

Mommy guilt is a powerful force and it takes a lot of support to kick it to the curb. No matter how many magazines, friends and family members say, "you will be a better mother if you take time for yourself," it still feels like we are bailing out on our responsibilities. But I really missed those good books. And adult conversation. And shopping without navigating a stroller and two kids who would rather be anywhere but in said stroller. Then something amazing happened.

I was volunteering with my church to produce an event that included a prayer walk and a Christian concert. Two days into the venture, the head of the committee said to me, "I have this feeling that you should emcee and sing in this event. Can you sing?"

YES!! said my heart. But then the questions started to creep into my head. *Who will watch the boys when I do this? Can I still do this?* It had been 10 years since I had sung a single note in front of anyone! *What will Dane think? Will he be supportive? Will my boys be okay if I spend less time with them?*

When I get caught in the spiral of self-doubt, I call the one person that pushes me beyond my own limits—my mom. She asked me all kinds of questions to lead me back to my heart. She did what moms do best—put the focus on me. By the end of the conversation I realized that I wouldn't be taking something away from my family by performing; I would be giving them a gift. I would be teaching them that you should always follow your passions and do something that pushes you out of your comfort zone.

Singing at the Christian concert–I'm on the left!

Fast forward five years and I am still singing with the praise band. We practice one night a week and it's the most restorative time for me. No matter how tired I am, my soul lights up as we sing songs to the Lord. The guilt is gone and thankfulness has replaced it. Maybe you don't have tiny persons to take care of in this season of your life. But you do have a demanding business that pulls you out of bed in the morning, whines to be taken care of, and keeps you from doing things that you really love. The guilt seeps in and takes hold when you see your spouse working diligently when you would rather head out for a bike ride with friends or take a hot bath. It's normal and natural to feel that way, but I want you to do everything you can to overcome it. Believe it or not, it will help your marriage.

"It can be especially good if each person in the power couple has his or her own sphere in which to rise up and each gains the other's respect for different talents," says Dr. Michael McNulty, a master trainer from the *Gottman Institute* and founder of the *Chicago Relationship Center.*

Your lives are so completely intertwined that it can be difficult to recognize each other's talents and abilities. Hobbies give you an opportunity to admire one another. A friend told me that she always felt a little torn when she left home right after dinner on Monday evenings to join her

Scrabble™ club, a group of about 10 women who played the game at a master's level for about two hours each week. One Monday she told her husband she wasn't going, thinking that he would appreciate her spending the evening with him for a change. He reacted with, "You should go! I want to watch *Antique Roadshow* any way." Hmmm, maybe a little time for his own interests was good for both of them, too. When she got home, he asked her if she had won her games. When she said yes, he told her he was proud of her and that he wished he could place a bet on her. She stopped feeling like she was taking something from him by giving something to herself.

When I give myself the opportunity to sing, I feel so alive. And, there is no better feeling than my husband saying, "Your song was amazing, babe. Really good." It feels even better because I'm passionate about worship and he sees that shining through me. I want that for you, too.

Make it Happen (15 Minutes)

I want you to have something that is just yours. I want it to give you an escape from the pressures of life. It doesn't have to be public; my mom always chooses to sew with sports on the TV as an escape. There's no right or wrong answer here; I would just ask that it's something that evokes emotion. Think about life before marriage or before the business. Were there things you loved to pursue? Are there bucket list items that you haven't had time to explore?

Here's a list from bplans.com of the top 10 hobbies of successful entrepreneurs to get your wheels turning:

- Competing in endurance events

- Playing video games
- Scuba diving
- Running
- Practicing yoga
- Traveling
- Doing creative home projects.
- Playing guitar and songwriting
- Gardening

Business owners are superior goal setters. Use that skill for you. Set a goal to learn something new or commit to getting back to doing something you love. Make a plan to fit it into your life. Schedule it. Stick to it. Embrace the joy it gives you.

DATING YOUR SPOUSE

"For husbands, this means love your wives, just as Christ loved the church. He gave up his life for her" (Ephesians 5:25).

Remember dating? Remember when you had butterflies in your stomach and you wanted to make sure to make the best impression possible? I do. My husband and I dated long distance for the first six months of our relationship and I would spend hours just packing my suitcase with the "perfect outfits." When I arrived, he would have the weekend completely planned from dinner reservations to coffee with friends he wanted me to meet. We made a major effort to impress each other and lit up in each other's presence. There was something magical about him being that focused on my every need and delighting in everything I said.

Romantic love changes over time; it becomes a background hum rather than an all-consuming need. We can easily become complacent. Everything else gets louder and more demanding. Crying babies, little league schedules, complaining clients, and looming deadlines overshadow the most important relationship that God has given us.

Dane and I went through a season where we didn't speak after the kids went to bed. We would collapse on our respective couches and binge watch HGTV and Food Network until we fell asleep. We weren't angry at each other. We were exhausted. Date nights slowly faded into a distant memory. *Redbook Magazine* tells me I'm not the only one. 50% of women say the No. 1 reason date night gets canceled is because they are too tired to go out. Half of us are too tired to have fun. That's craziness!

I wish I could say that all that television somehow helped us feel more rested but it had the opposite effect. I began to feel disconnected. When we did have time together, I couldn't really think of anything meaningful to say. I wondered what he was thinking about and going through other than the things that I could see from the outside. It didn't matter that I spent most of my time with him; I missed him.

Valentine's Day was coming up and I spent a lot of time trying to come up with something meaningful. My Godmother has said to me that the best gift you can give someone is a memory and I decided to use that wisdom to grow our marriage. I catalogued our "bucket list" of things we had always talked about doing together and then scoured Groupon for more ideas. I wanted more adventure, more fun in our life. I finalized the list with things like paddle boarding lessons, swimming with dolphins, hiking Myakka State Park, a brewery tour, a date night in the pool with a bottle of wine, and more. The grand finale was a weekend away on Sanibel Island for the next Valentine's Day. I made a card for each month, and I wrote a short note about the adventure on each one. The envelope was labeled for the month and he wasn't allowed to open it until the first of the month.

"Really?! A date night every month? You planned all this?" he said as he opened up the first envelope. "So, what kind of stuff is in here?"

"Can't tell. It's a surprise." I smiled, thankful for his curiosity and enthusiasm.

"What about babysitters?" said my ever-practical husband.

"Done. Mom is scheduled to come every month. We just have to tell her the weekend."

He smiled and hugged me then, fully receiving the gift.

Those activities shifted our lives in a way that is difficult to put into words. We were still tired, but the date night was invigorating. We laughed, we learned new things together, we remembered why we love each other so very much.

Other couples have found creative ways to handle this as well. According to Business Insider.com, Facebook's Mark Zuckerberg "drew up a relationship agreement with his then-girlfriend and now-wife Priscilla Chan when she moved to Palo Alto, California, several years ago. In it, he agreed to take her on a date once a week and spend 100 minutes of alone time each week with her outside the office or his apartment." (Do you think they use a stopwatch?)

"We go out every Friday night, no matter what," shared a couple from our church. "We're still dating after 30 years." I love that. Intentionality is the key. Whether you can fit in a date night once a month or once a week, you have to fit it in. You manage to schedule back-to-back meetings, don't you? You muster the energy to tackle that proposal at 10 PM, right? Your marriage deserves that same level of dedication and follow-through.

"To get the full value of joy, you must have someone to divide it with," said Mark Twain.

Let's start getting the full value of joy.

Make it Happen (20 Minutes)

It's time to make your date night bucket list. You can only list "out to dinner" and "go to the movies" if there is a fun twist. Is it a new restaurant you've really wanted to try? Is the movie a drive-in movie? Change it up. The point is to get out of your comfort zone and try new things together. If you are stuck, Groupon or Living Social always have fun (and cheap!) experiences to try out. I would also recommend the book, *52 Uncommon Dates*, by Christopher Hudson for some creative ideas that will bring you closer.

Next, you need to schedule it. Pretend like you have a monthly (or weekly!) consulting engagement. Move things if you must and make this night with your spouse a number one priority. Book the sitter, set aside the cash and plan to run through Starbucks on the way if the "too tired" excuse pops up. You're going on this date. Got it?

Lastly, remember what it's like to have fun. Leave work at work. There's no need to use this time for hashing out strategy. (I can't imagine you'll have time to do that as you pull on wet suits for your snorkeling adventure but I know it's tempting.) Laugh, please. A lot. Flirt, kiss, hold hands and remember how lucky you are to live this life together.

INTENTIONAL FAMILY TIME

God tells us in Proverbs 22:6 to "Start children off on the way they should go, and even when they are old they will not turn from it."

I can see my childhood evenings in my mind, constantly repeating themselves like the movie *Groundhog Day*. My mom would be home when we got home from school and have a snack ready for us. (I learned later that she would have to actually kick people out of her office every day to make that happen.) We would talk to her about our day, play, and then she would start dinner. My sister and I would take out pots and pans and spin around the kitchen talking to my mom. My dad would come home, take off his shoes and lay them on the brown linoleum tile floor. "What's for dinner, Beck?" he would ask without fail.

We all piled to the table and my dad would start talking about something they were dealing with at the office. He would talk and talk and talk and my sister and I would start playing footsie under the table or retreating into our own imaginations. My mom tried valiantly to have him cut off his stories or include us in the conversation. Sometimes it worked. Most of the time it didn't. He would tell her how great dinner was and then head to his recliner to watch the news. And that was the end of our daily interaction with our dad.

My mom wasn't about to let this continue. She has a fierce determination in her and she decided to get creative. "I knew if I just got him away from the office, he would be able to reconnect. I had this crazy idea to buy a cabin. I had grown up with a cabin at the Ozarks so I floated the idea to Dad. He had no idea of my ulterior motive. Thankfully, he was on board right away," she shared.

The cabin was an hour away from our house on Atwood Lake. It was what you might call a "fixer-upper" but we didn't care. It had log beams and threadbare carpet that had seen years of muddy footprints, but it felt more like a home than our "real" house. It was a place that invited kids with damp bathing suits to curl up on the old couch to watch a movie; a place that we could all let our hair down and live freely. That cabin holds the best memories of my childhood. It was where my dad finally got his head out of work and started being a father. He taught me how to ski, how to drive a boat, and how to swim in those waters. We went to the apple festival in the fall and on hikes during the winter. The cabin gave us the chance to really get to know him and I'll treasure that always.

I recently told him how thankful I was for that decision and then I asked a question that had been on my mind awhile. I asked him why he couldn't just hang out with us at home.

"I couldn't disconnect otherwise," my dad explained to me. "If we were at home, I could just head over to the office on a Saturday. But I couldn't work at the lake—that was before internet or even cable went out that far. Mom and I knew we had to do something drastic."

It may be time for you to do something drastic as well.

"The time parents spend with children is regarded as critical for positive cognitive, behavioral and academic outcomes," says Judith Treas, UCI Chancellor's Professor of sociology and co-author of a study comparing child care time across 11 Western countries between 1965 and 2012. "College-educated moms spent an estimated 123 minutes daily on child care. Fathers with a college degree spent about 74 minutes a day with their kids."

That may seem reasonable until you hear this statistic. The National Institute of Health's Medline Plus reports that, "The average kid spends three hours per day watching television and five to seven hours total on screens." They spend about an hour and a half with parents, and seven hours with screens. What is going to yield the most influence?

It can be tempting to hand them a device when we need to catch up on emails. We're busy. It's a win/win right? Not necessarily. As a child of a power couple I can tell you that I only wanted some quality time. A walk, a board game, or a puzzle was all it took to feel connected to my parents. I can attest that this is not easy in the digital age we live in today.

Even if my phone is put away, my watch notifies me of a pressing email or a text that demands my immediate response. I have heard my kids say more than once, "Mommy! Put down your phone!" I have had to put up physical boundaries while I intentionally spend time with the kids (the watch and the phone get put in the other room) as well as mental boundaries. I ask myself if I would stop a meeting with my most important client to send a text message or peruse my emails as they are talking. Never! And yet, I found myself doing that all the time with my children. They are much more important than any client.

Make it Happen (10 Minutes)

You are the one, with God's help, that will show them how to live. You have the opportunity to show them that they are a true blessing from the Lord through your actions. It's a decision. You must be intentional about it. "Fathers, do not exasperate your children; instead, bring them up in the training and instruction of the Lord" (Ephesians 6:4).

So how can we stop "exasperating our children"? Here are a few tried and true ways from my family to yours:

1. **Set Aside Ten Minutes a Day per Child to do Something of Their Choosing.**

   Kids understand passion. The things they are passionate about don't always match up with the things we care about (Minecraft, anyone?), but we have to make an effort to be a part of their world. It opens up this beautiful opportunity to connect with them at their level.

   My middle child loves sports. I am terrible at sports. (If I catch a ball he has thrown, I actually celebrate a little inside.) And we live in Florida and I sweat just walking to my car. Playing outside feels similar to torture. Still, I try to always say *yes* when my sweet boy wants to play baseball or soccer or street hockey, or all three.

   Something amazing happens when I say yes. He lights up, gets all the equipment together and he begins to lead. He coaches me. He encourages me. He tells me things I didn't know about him because he finally has a moment without his brother and sister constantly interrupting him. Do I get sweaty and miss 8/10 catches? Absolutely. But I wouldn't trade that time with him for anything.

2. **Tell Family Stories. Often.**

Kids are funny. Really funny. They also have this amazing gift of being able to laugh at themselves. Stories make them feel treasured and important. They are the fabric that makes your family completely unique. Set aside a night to sit around the kitchen table telling some of your favorites. Plan on your stories spurring on more, "Do you remember that time when…" from other family members. Here's a story from our family archives to get you in the mood to giggle.

When my oldest was four, it was his job to walk our 12-year-old pug/beagle mix. Walking him consisted of going right in front of our house and letting the dog do his business on the patch of grass near the sidewalk. On this particular day, Luke took the dog out as usual, then, minutes later, busted through the front door frantic and without our dog. "Buddy! Are you okay? Where's Burton?" my husband asked.

"He's with the neighbor! I need a towel!" he said as he pushed past us toward the dish towel drawer.

Questions abounded but we held our tongues as we peeked out the front door. Sure enough, a neighbor we had never met was holding our dog's leash looking just as bewildered as we were.

"Wait, why do you need a towel?" I asked.

"Because! I peed on Burton!"

"You what!?"

"He was peeing and it made me have to pee so I just started to pee on the tree and then he was done and he walked right through my pee and now he's soaking wet!" He told us this as if this sequence of events made even a tiny bit of logical sense.

We tried to stifle our laughter as we relieved (no pun intended) the neighbor from dog-sitting and introduced ourselves as the parents of the kid who just peed on the dog. You just can't make this stuff up.

3. **Fill Their Bucket**

Make time once a day to "fill each other's buckets." We choose dinner time but you can do it on the way to school or right before bedtime. Just make sure it's a time when everyone is together. You simply choose one person to honor, then go around the table giving each person an opportunity to share what they love or admire about them. But don't be discouraged if it's a slow start. At first, we got answers like, "I love you because you eat tacos," but as we practiced this ritual, my children began to understand.

"What do you love about Daddy?" I asked my oldest son, praying that he didn't answer "noodles" like his sister just had.

He looked at my husband shyly then looked away, thinking. "Well, I love how Daddy always fixes everything that is broken.

No matter what, he stops and fixes my stuff. Even when my heart is broken, he does his best to fix it."

I stopped mid-bite and locked eyes with my husband. We were both misty-eyed and moved by our son's beautiful words. "Buddy," he began, "that was the best yet. That made me cry." Our son jumped up to hug him, then just as quickly ran back to his seat. It was clear that he was proud and my husband and I were overcome with the gift of our little boy's perspective.

I know that sometimes we institute rituals in our families and they seem to be a lot of work without much return. We think our kids don't even notice or that it isn't really making as much of an impact as we hoped. Our efforts are never wasted. Each conversation shapes their character, whether we know it or not. The parenting game is not one for quick rewards but it certainly pays big in the long run.

THE ANTI-ADULTERY PLAN

"Marriage should be honored by all, and the marriage bed kept pure, for God will judge the adulterer and all the sexually immoral" (Hebrews 13:4).

"Lots of people see this as a divine buzzkill," my pastor shared in a sermon on boundaries. We giggled a little, knowing he was right. "But it's not! God knows us and wants to protect us."

Right again.

The prevailing message in society today is, *if it feels good, do it*! It's easy to know what we want. The world tells us not to settle for anything less and then insists that we deserve more. And yet, as we seek our own fulfillment, we become immersed in ourselves. We buy into the lie that selfishness is necessary and forget that "feeling good" can and will dramatically impact those we love. Temptation is real and we need the help of the supernatural to overcome it. The consequences of chasing fulfillment outside of marriage are dire.

I interviewed an entrepreneurial couple that had rebuilt their marriage after an affair had nearly destroyed it. We sat in their beautifully appointed living room that featured a wall of smiling children and grandchildren. You would never have guessed that there had been a hiccup, let alone an earthquake in their marriage. But as the story unfolded, the pain flashed in her eyes. "He was traveling a lot for work and…let's just say, he didn't act like a Christian man."

Her husband dropped his head, unable to meet my eye.

"We had to get into Christian counseling for that one because there was no trust! None!" she continued. "We went to separate counselors, then went to counseling together. Took a long time."

He nodded in agreement, then added, "My counselor told me something. He said to me, 'It took years to walk into those woods. It's going to take just as long to walk out of them.' That was a hard one to hear but he was right."

I asked her how she forgave him. She said something beautiful: "Jesus showed me how."

John 8:3-11 tells us the character of our savior.

The teachers of the law and the Pharisees brought in a woman caught in adultery. They made her stand before the group and said to Jesus, "Teacher, this woman was caught in the act of adultery. In the Law Moses commanded us to stone such women. Now what do you say?" They were using this question as a trap, in order to have a basis for accusing him.

But Jesus bent down and started to write on the ground with his finger. When they kept on questioning him, he straightened up and said to them, "Let any one of you who is without sin be the first to throw a stone at her." Again he stooped down and wrote on the ground.

At this, those who heard began to go away one at a time, the older ones first, until only Jesus was left, with the woman still standing there. Jesus straightened up and asked her, "Woman, where are they? Has no one condemned you?"

"No one, sir," she said.

"Then neither do I condemn you," Jesus declared. "Go now and leave your life of sin."

Jesus does not condemn us. He calls us to righteousness. He is not quick to judgment. He's not a finger-pointer. He loves you. If you have crossed the boundary, stop and live a life that honors God. To repent means to break the chain of sin and literally go in the opposite direction. He tells us that, "It is God's will that you should be sanctified: that you should avoid sexual immorality; that each of you should learn to control your own body in a way that is holy and honorable" (Thessalonians 4:3-4). You can ask for His help and He will give you his strength.

If you have been devastated by your partner committing adultery, I pray that you are able to drop your stones. I pray that you can find a strong Christian counselor that can help lead both you and your partner out of the deep dark woods. Trust is not immediately reinstated; it is built through consistent behavior over time. Ask God for patience as you go through this journey.

Make it Happen (30 Minutes)

Temptation is powerful but God is stronger. Our marriages need some fences designed by the greatest engineer in the world. We are given building instructions in His word that, if followed, are foolproof.

1. **Guard Your Body and Your Mind.**

   "You have heard that the law of Moses says, 'Do not commit adultery.' But I say, anyone who even looks at a woman with lust in his eye has already committed adultery with her in his heart." Jesus gives us this hard truth in Matthew 5:27-28.

   Wow. This is increasingly difficult in a sex-filled culture.

   We went to the beach the other day and I saw more 20-something butt cheeks than I care to mention. I'm no prude; I love a cute bikini but these girls were barely covering their nether regions. I said something to my husband and he said, "Those girls have got nothing on you."

   I didn't even realize I was feeling insecure about it until he said that simple sentence. I needed to know that he only had eyes for me. Keep your eyes on each other.

   Hillsong's "Not Today" gives us really cool lyrics that serve as a prayer when we are tempted.

   I'm standing on Jesus' name
   So let the devil know not today
   Let the devil know not today No no

Not now not ever again Jesus
Let the devil know not today

It is a fight. But it's a fight that Jesus has already won for us. Turn to Him and He will fill your spirit with His goodness and light and rid you of the devil's temptations. Let the devil know—not today.

2. **Recognize the Lie**

It is said that, "the grass is always greener on the other side." The Bible tells us that this little cliché applies perfectly to adultery. "A prostitute will bring you to poverty, but sleeping with another man's wife may cost you your very life. Can a man scoop fire into his lap and not be burned? Can he walk on hot coals and not blister his feet? So it is with the man who sleeps with another man's wife. He who embraces her will not go unpunished. But the man who commits adultery is an utter fool, for he destroys his own soul" (Proverbs 6:26-32).

Those are some strong words from a God who loves us enough to die for us. I know I have used harsh language like that with my children when I try to protect them. "Look before you cross the street or you will be hit by a car. This is important! The car could kill you." They look at me with a glimmer of doubt in their eyes. Would it *really* be that bad, they ask. Yes, it could be that bad.

Sleeping with another man may seem like the perfect salve to your pain. This person "gets you" and provides a safe harbor in the midst of the storms of your real life. If you haven't been having date nights with your husband, you can feel attention-starved, even unwanted. Another man is complimentary and makes you start thinking it would be a good idea to have a little fun for a change. This is a lie. Do not believe it. It can feel as compelling as a drink of seawater to a stranded sailor on a lifeboat. He is parched. He knows it would be a huge mistake, probably fatal, to fill his mouth and sooth his throat with the cool ocean. The strong ones don't give in, and they survive. Giving in to adultery may quench a thirst for the moment, and then it will cost you your life as you know it.

If your marriage is at the point where the arms of another seem to be the only solution, run to the arms of your Savior. Your church (or one nearby) probably has dozens of resources to help your marriage heal. They can lead you to certified Christian counselors, small groups, books and devotionals. They can shine a light on the truth. Your urge will pass, with God's help. You won't always feel so unhappy and on the brink of giving into temptation. You can get through it faster than you realize if you seek help.

Are you believing lies today? Recognize them and ask God to reveal His truth. Seek out resources to help you if you cannot see a way out.

3. **Build the Fences / Railings /Boundaries**

Dane and I had to have a contentious conversation once about a close friend of his. She was single, beautiful, and completely opposite of me. She pushed every button of insecurity in my bones because I feared he really wanted someone like her. When I asked him not to be alone with her, he felt as if I was saying I didn't trust him. I did trust him; I just didn't want him to be presented with the opportunity. Eventually, his heart opened and we agreed that he wouldn't be alone with her. That one statement made me feel safe.

Vice President Mike Pence made national headlines when he shared the fence he and his wife had built. He will not have dinner with another woman alone, nor will he attend an event with alcohol without her there. Critics abounded on social media as people called it discriminatory against women. Debra S. Katz, an employment discrimination attorney, told the *Atlantic*, "I can see many reasons why this is a terrible idea, terrible in the sense of discriminatory."

Elite Daily writes, "Pence's alleged eating choices are not just strange and sexist, they're also legally discriminatory."

The world will fight you on this. It will feel unreasonable and uncomfortable to ask for the things your heart is saying your marriage needs. I challenge both of you to shut out all the outside voices and ask God what fences He would like you to build. Explore the Bible, spend time in prayer. You may be perfectly comfortable with your spouse going out to dinner with someone, but not with them going to that person's house without you. Say it. Start the conversation.

Marriage Boundaries

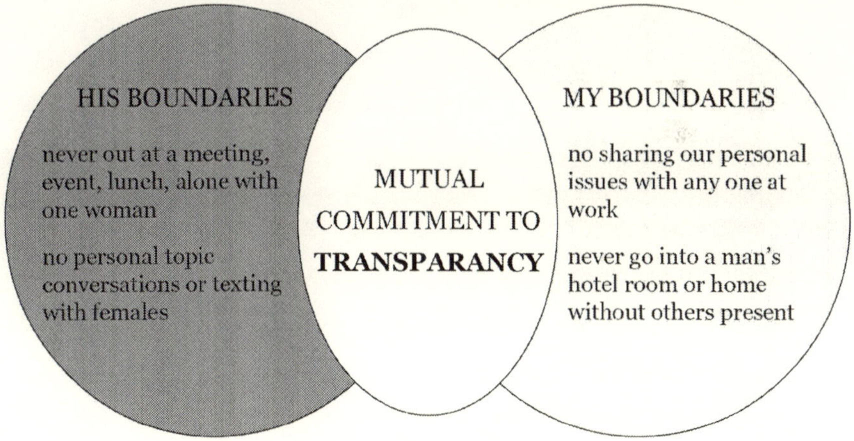

Diagram 4.0

There will be things that you don't agree on. You will feel as if your husband is saying that you aren't devoted or that you can't handle yourself. I ask you to drop your defensiveness. Setting aside six months of bills in your savings account does not mean your husband doesn't believe the business will provide. It's a back-up; it's a smart safety measure. This is too. Approach this as a way to protect the one you love the most.

Finally, agree. This conversation cannot be closed until both of you are on the same page. Confirm verbally what you understand and have your partner agree. Seal it with a kiss.

5

I'll Do My Job, You Do Yours

Whatever you do, do it with all your heart,
as working for the Lord, not for human masters.

Colossians 3:23

DEFINING AND AGREEING ON RESPONSIBILITIES

Imagine walking into a new job and being told to do whatever needs done. Anything at all. As you glance around the busy office trying to ignore your sweaty palms, you notice that there's an empty seat in the accounting department. You sit down and decide to start running the accounts payable. Suddenly, someone taps you on the shoulder and asks you to join the sales meeting. After five minutes, a head peaks in the door to inform you that there is an issue in the programming department, so you sit down at a computer to figure out why the software isn't running as expected. That sounds crazy, right? You would be so stressed out trying to figure out if you were doing enough or doing the important things, wishing you didn't have to be a mind reader. Meanwhile, the people counting on you would probably be sorely disappointed that you were not meeting their expectations.

That scenario sounds ridiculous, doesn't it? Who would do that to a new hire? And yet, that's exactly what entrepreneurs do to themselves. We have an "if we don't do it, no one will," attitude and sometimes that's exactly what you need to get our businesses off the ground. But we can't sustain that pace. If we have every job from janitor to CEO, we constantly step on each other's toes and find ourselves quarreling over who did or didn't get something done.

This is not a new problem. Moses, in a sense, was running a huge enterprise as he worked to organize the Jewish people that have just been freed from slavery after 400 years. They were without the familiar boundaries and rules of slavery and suddenly found themselves arguing over…well…everything. The people came directly to Moses to solve every single problem and dispute. He spent all day every day dealing with problems and he was beginning to feel overwhelmed.

"Moses' father-in-law said, 'This is no way to go about it. You'll burn out, and the people right along with you. This is way too much for you—you can't do this alone. Now listen to me. Let me tell you how to do this so that God will be in this with you. Be there for the people before God, but let the matters of concern be presented to God. Your job is to teach them the rules and instructions, to show them how to live, what to do. And then you need to keep a sharp eye out for competent men—men who fear God, men of integrity, men who are incorruptible—and appoint them as leaders over groups organized by the thousand, by the hundred, by fifty, and by ten. They'll be responsible for the everyday work of judging among the people. They'll bring the hard cases to you, but in the routine cases they'll be the judges. They will share your load and that will make it easier for you. If you handle the work this way, you'll have the strength to carry out whatever God commands you, and the people in their settings will flourish also.'" (Exodus 18:17-23 MSG)

You'll burn out.

This is too much for you.

You can't do this alone.

They will share your load and that will make it easier for you.

I know it feels impossible to "share your load" right now. It feels better to have your hands in everything. It seems easier to just handle it yourself. Whether at work, at home, or in your relationship, there is nothing more crucial than to delegate and communicate clear roles and expectations. It saves you from burn out. It frees you to focus on your strengths and allows your partner to do the same. When others share our load, it does indeed make it easier for us. The first step toward gaining freedom is to define responsibilities but it is often done in a broad way. What does it really mean to do "the accounting"? Does that mean they handle everything from payroll to taxes in-house, or are some areas outsourced? Are there some responsibilities that are shared? The grey area is fertile ground for miscommunication and mistrust. As someone once said,

"When you start to wonder whether you can trust someone or not, that is when you already know you don't."

My husband and I coach couples that are ready to build more value in their business. They come to us hopeful and optimistic, but also a bit fearful. Growth, to them, means increased responsibility and more opportunities to argue. They are so embroiled in the day-to-day that they can't see how they can add any more to their plate.

"Did you…" statements tend to plague the couples that come to us for help because they are lacking in clarity. "Did you follow-up on that proposal?" or "Did you get those reports done for the meeting?" or even, "Did you remember to buy toilet paper?" Sometimes these are helpful; they are useful when you have agreed to hold each other accountable. But most of the time they end up grating on the other person and escalating the friction of the interaction.

We met with a client that had a cleaning business and her husband was affronted by her consistent lack of trust in him. The company was her baby more than his; her emotions were completely invested. Details were important to her and everything had to be handled according to procedure. Her husband, however, felt smothered. "I'm supposed to handle existing client relationships but she's always breathing down my neck," he shared in an interview. "It's like she doesn't think I'll really do it."

She snapped to attention. "If I don't follow up, it won't get done!"

He shrugged his shoulders as if to say, *See. I told you.*

Ultimately, she didn't trust him to get it done. He failed before he had even begun. She felt it was her responsibility to manage him. He felt that his role was autonomous and her management was eroding their trust for one another. This became a constant underlying tension between them.

Once we explore this further, we find that roles are often assigned by default rather than agreed upon. *Agreeing* implies that we have the same opinion about something. We have talked about responsibilities and decided what each of us should be doing *together*. *Assigning* simply means that one of us has designated that role to the other without any discussion. You may have assumed that your husband knows your expectations or vice versa. This simply cannot happen in a marriage or a business partnership if your long-term vision of success is to be fulfilled.

"Well, he wants me to do the accounting and the marketing," a client said sharply during an interview on job responsibilities. She leaned back against the conference room chair and crossed her arms. It was clearly a battle position.

"Are you currently doing accounting and marketing?" I asked.

"Yeah, but only because he wants me to. He's outsourced all the jobs I enjoy." Her shoulders slumped in defeat as she looked up, hoping that we could help her untangle this mess.

What part of that sounds like an agreement? None of it. She was angry and disillusioned with her husband and the business. She was defeated and well on her way to burn out. It's not enough to define responsibilities—you and your spouse must agree on them. But wait…there's more.

We worked with a couple that had done a beautiful job defining and agreeing to responsibilities but they struggled with respecting those mutually-defined boundaries. They had decided early on that she would be the CEO while he offered IT support, resources and advice. He was an avid reader and able to retain virtually everything he read. He was a fountain of business knowledge. She was open to all of his insights but they had become overwhelming.

"You just gotta get more locations. That's it. Problem solved," he said.

"But I'm not asking you to fix this," she replied, frustration creeping into her voice.

"But the solution is right there in front of you!" He said as he threw up his arms in exasperation.

"I guess," she said quietly.

Clearly she was worn down. She didn't even continue to fight him on it. She was seeking collaboration. She didn't need him to do her job for her. When we dove a bit deeper he shared that he "was only trying to help," and she was able to share that it hurt her confidence each time he told her to go another direction.

Can you see how a lack of clarity of expectations, agreements, and communication had become a fortified roadblock to this couple's effective partnership?

The Bible does a beautiful job of clearly listing the responsibilities of a "wife of noble character." A note of caution: This is not to be read as a "to-do" list of a Christian woman. I do not want you closing this book to start a Pinterest board filled with "5 Easy Steps to Planting a Vineyard." We are called by God to be women of valor and wisdom. This is simply one example of what that looks like:

Proverbs 31

A wife of noble character who can find?

She is worth far more than rubies.
Her husband has full confidence in her
and lacks nothing of value.

She brings him good, not harm,
all the days of her life.

She selects wool and flax
and works with eager hands.

She is like the merchant ships,
bringing her food from afar.

She gets up while it is still night;
she provides food for her family
and portions for her female servants.

She considers a field and buys it;
out of her earnings she plants a vineyard.

She sets about her work vigorously;
her arms are strong for her tasks.

She sees that her trading is profitable,
and her lamp does not go out at night. In her hand she holds the distaff and grasps the spindle with her fingers.

She opens her arms to the poor
and extends her hands to the needy.

When it snows, she has no fear for her household;
for all of them are clothed in scarlet.

She makes coverings for her bed;
she is clothed in fine linen and purple.

Her husband is respected at the city gate,
where he takes his seat among the elders of the land. She makes
linen garments and sells them,
and supplies the merchants with sashes.

She is clothed with strength and dignity;
she can laugh at the days to come.

She speaks with wisdom,
and faithful instruction is on her tongue.

She watches over the affairs of her household
and does not eat the bread of idleness.

Her children arise and call her blessed;
her husband also, and he praises her:

"Many women do noble things,
but you surpass them all."

Charm is deceptive, and beauty is fleeting;
but a woman who fears the Lord is to be praised.

Honor her for all that her hands have done,
and let her works bring her praise at the city gate.

I'm exhausted just thinking about how much that woman does! I wonder if your spouse might be amazed when you give a list of all the things that you currently do. I have a feeling that you will be amazed by each other.

Make it Happen (30 Minutes)

I'd like you to take five or ten minutes to list out all the jobs you do at the office. Everything. If you take out the trash and scrub the toilets in-between conference calls, it should be on the list. Next, make a list of everything you see your spouse doing. You may not ask them what they do, just list out what you notice from day to day.

I have created a blank Venn diagram for you to gain a visual perspective of your responsibilities. If there is something that you both do, write it in the overlapping section. I have a feeling you are going to need some big circles. Here's a mini example:

Job Responsibilities

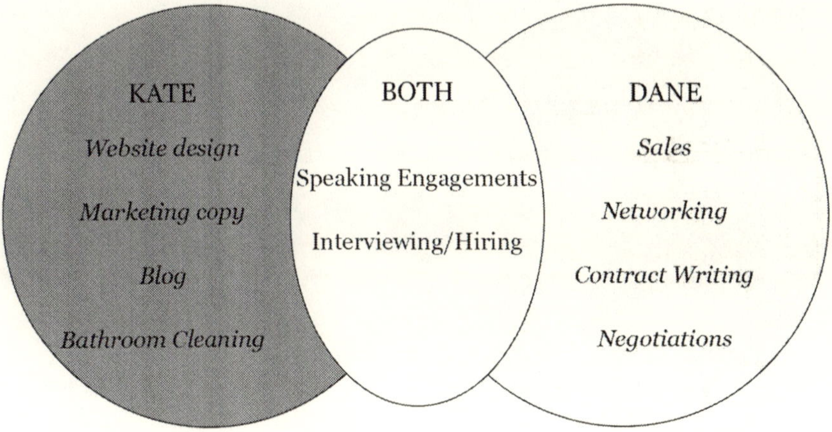

Diagram 5.0

Next, sit down together with both lists handy and get ready to be impressed by each other. Compare your diagrams. Are areas of miscommunication present? Does he think he's supposed to be doing something you are already doing? Make a note of them to come back to in a minute.

Are you amazed by all he does? Tell him. Take this moment to thank him for taking on the lion's share of the work in those areas of the business where he owns the job.

Are there areas where you overlap? Sometimes this makes sense. Check out this example from Jessie Randall, co-founder of indie shoe and handbag brand, Loeffler Randall. "Brian and I have really complementary skill sets," she said. "I've always headed up creative and design. He really runs the business, oversees e-commerce and sales. The one place where we work together is marketing."

The word *complementary* is key here. You each have clear strengths and weaknesses. I am very creative while my husband is a detail guy. If we shared the marketing responsibilities…well, let's just say that wouldn't work out so well. We had to sit down and do a SWOT analysis to figure some of it out. The SWOT process is used by companies, educators, and anyone who wants to better understand their Strengths and Weaknesses, see what Opportunities are open to them, and what Threats they face. Now it's your turn to give it a shot. Here are the steps:

1. **Strengths**

    - What are your natural God-given strengths?
    - What values do you embrace that make you unique?
    - Where does your training and expertise lie?

- What network of people or resources is available to you?
- What strengths do other people recognize in you?

2. **Weaknesses**
    - What tasks intimidate you?
    - What are you most likely to avoid?
    - What weaknesses are pointed out to you by others?
    - What areas of training or education need to be improved?

3. **Opportunities**
    - What new direction is the company taking or considering?
    - Is there a demand or gap that requires your skills?
    - What are the biggest changes coming in your industry or company?
    - Where do your skill sets dovetail with this new area?

4. **Threats**
    - What is the biggest external threat to your success?
    - Do you have any past failures that could affect you? How can you learn from that experience?
    - What are the chronic tolerations/things that keep being put up with but not resolved?

Place each of your answers in a grid. Here's a sample:

Kate's SWOT Matrix

STRENGTHS	WEAKNESSES
Public Speaking Marketing People Skills Structure/Process Design	Sales Math/Accounting Product Knowledge
OPPORTUNITES	**THREATS**
Seminars Client Networking Re-Branding/Maintaining Brand	Family Demands Lack of Follow-through

Bring out your Venn diagram and SWOT analysis. Are there areas that you are responsible for that do not fit into your skill set? Do they fall into your spouse's Strengths or Opportunities? Consider and discuss reassigning them for better results. There will be some that don't fall into either of your abilities. Make a solid list of them and do one of three things: assign it to an employee, outsource it, or get the training you need to get it done. The first two are ideal but only if you can currently afford it. No need to get into a bunch of debt, right? There will be a time when you can hire and manage someone that does all of these things but that time may not be now. That being said, you won't be effective if you and your spouse don't delegate as much as possible so you can focus on what no one else can do—build and grow a highly profitable business.

Are there new areas you want to explore that fall right into your wheelhouse? Wonderful! Write them down to dig deep later. In Chapter 8, you will learn some great strategies for making them happen.

Lastly, get to work on a real job description. Approach this task with the same gusto you would with a new hire. List out everything you have agreed on, including a hierarchy. Who is the boss of each responsibility? Are you the final say? Would you rather go through some type of approval process? It's time to get it on paper. Share your final draft with your spouse and be open to their edits. This is something you must both be comfortable with before it's put into action. When the final edits are completed and executed, print a copy of both job descriptions and keep them handy. Use them to assign new tasks and to hold each other accountable.

You'll want to agree on how "holding each other accountable" should look. Do you meet briefly each morning and update the task/accountability list? Is there an online project management system that would be the best tool for you both to use? What are your agreed-upon boundaries about *how* and *how not* to follow up with one another?

FROM CRITICISM TO RECOGNITION

"The words of the reckless pierce like swords, but the tongue of the wise brings healing" (Proverbs 12:18).

While you may have defined and agreed on responsibilities (Congrats!), you may struggle to give up control. Too much is riding on everything working like a fine-tuned machine. You're both relying on this business and each other to pay for your home, your clothing, your food, your cars…everything. If your partner messes up, you could lose…everything. But that fear can manifest itself in ugly ways.

Remember when we talked about our expectations as young brides? This doesn't end at the altar. New expectations as a business owner and wife are being born every day and yet we often fail to communicate them to each other. We expect them to be spending their time growing a new product line and every time we see them doing something else, we feel anger rising up. They expect us to focus half our time on marketing and half our time on sales but you thought you were only doing marketing on a project basis. Resentment grows under the surface and erupts at the most inopportune time.

Snide comments can start to infiltrate your conversations. Words like, "You just aren't committed to this project," or "That wouldn't have happened if that was really important to you," cut deep. Our tongues are the most powerful muscle and can inflict more lasting pain than any other part of our body. Physical wounds heal but mental wounds linger and fester, especially when the words come from someone who is supposed to love and honor us.

It's one thing to be an accountability partner that provides constructive criticism—it's another thing to be the one that breaks down your partner's self-esteem by pointing out their flaws and failures with judgment. Constructive criticism is an essential element in a marriage and a business partnership. We all need someone who will help us see what is in our blind spots or push us beyond our own imagined capabilities. Constant criticism, however, erodes trust and creates conflict.

Are you more prone to fight or flight? When we are criticized, we react in one of two ways. Our response can be passive. We may deem their comment unworthy of a response and ignore it completely. We push the criticism away, maybe because we dismiss it or sometimes because we know it's valid but would rather run from it. The other is defensive. We spout accusations back at our accuser and vigorously disagree. "But whether passive or aggressive, defensiveness tends only to escalate the conflict," explains Terry Hargrave in *Essential Humility in Marriage*. "If spouses feel that their frustrations and complaints are not being addressed, their frustration and anger grows, resulting in further criticism and expressions of contempt. When defensiveness becomes a pattern in marriages, I believe that is a sure sign that trustworthiness has deteriorated to a critical point."

It's embarrassing to fail. It hits our confidence and temporarily debilitates us. We internalize it and begin to believe the voice in our head that says things like, *You are never going to succeed*, or, *You don't even know what you're doing*. Admitting your own failures takes great courage but giving grace to your husband for their failures takes God's love and grace.

"When you give your spouse the freedom to fail, you begin to remove the pressure to perform for acceptance," writes Dennis Rainey on FamilyLife.com. "You free your mate to take risks and try again. You free him to excel. Failure then becomes a tutor, not a judge. In the presence of freedom, we learn from failures instead of being intimidated by them. In the absence of condemnation, confidence in how God can use you mounts." We need our spouses to lift us up with truth and remind us that we are not a failure because we failed. You are only a failure if you stop trying. You glorify God when you pray through a difficult disappointment and place your trust in God's sovereign will. Both of you want success in your marriage and your business. When your spouse does something that hinders either of those end goals, we have an opportunity to choose criticism or grace.

If either of you are saying or thinking that the other one isn't cutting it, it's time for a conversation that will help you define the conditions of satisfaction. *Conditions of Satisfaction are the acceptance criteria that clarify the desired behavior.* Put simply, this is a way to communicate and agree on your expectations so that you stop getting so nasty with each other, and put an end to unfulfilled expectations caused by a lack of clarity.

Here is an example of a conversation which eventually defined agreed-upon Conditions of Satisfaction:

> "We haven't gone out to lunch in a long time."
>
> "True. When do you want to go?"
>
> "Any day. You're the one who is always too busy."
>
> "I can make time to have lunch with you any day but Wednesday. What day works for you?"
>
> "How about Friday?"
>
> "Yes, Friday works fine. What time?"
>
> "I'll be out so I'll meet you at noon."
>
> "Sounds good. Where should we meet?"
>
> "I don't know, you pick."
>
> "How about Café Baci?"

"Sure. Put it on your calendar so you don't forget. Friday, noon, Café Baci."

"Great! Thanks for thinking of having lunch together. I'm looking forward to it."

"Let's do it every Friday, same time, same place."

"Okay, that sounds perfect."

Now, here is the condensed essentials-only version:

Request: "Will you meet me for lunch on Wednesday at noon at Café Baci?"

[contains all essentials of Condition of Satisfaction – who, what, when, where]

Counter Offer: "I must decline that request, but if it's Friday at noon at Café Baci, yes."

[She could not meet one of the Conditions of Satisfaction (the day, Wednesday), so she chose to make a counter-offer. This is actually a new request, and thus must be accepted, declined, or countered.]

Accepter: "Yes, I agree to lunch with you, Friday, noon, at Café Baci."

Agreement: "I agree to all your Conditions of Satisfaction. I promise to be there."

The above example sounds too formal, not like normal conversation, but let me tell you—whenever there is a topic that is a bit sticky, or emotionally charged (you know the ones), being super clear on each of your Requests, Conditions of Satisfaction, and Promises cuts through the jungle of thorny, emotional entanglements. Clear communication is the number one way to prevent heart problems....meaning, problems that erode your loving, successful partnership.

Make it Happen (10 Minutes)

Criticism is almost always rooted in fear or insecurity. They own those feelings and do not have the right to reassign them to you. But that can't happen unless those emotions are uncovered and named. If you have noticed the same criticism coming up over and over again, I guarantee it's from an expectation that hasn't been met. I've outlined a three step process that will save you from many arguments at home and at work.

Here's your job during this interaction: Drop your defenses completely. This isn't about what kind of job you are doing. This is about clarifying expectations. That's your goal. Focus on solving that problem rather than defending yourself. You've got this!

Note: This is an oversimplified example. Your conversation will likely have many more twists and turns. Don't lose heart. The two of you will learn how to get to the crux of the issue faster as you practice.

1. **Ask the Person to Verbalize the Problem.**

   "I've noticed that you seem upset about the amount of time I spend on marketing. Please tell me your expectations."

They will wiggle. They will be vague. They will try to brush it off three different ways. They may say something like, "You just don't seem committed."

It will burn. You will want to chase after that red flag waving. Don't do it. Dig deeper until you get something real. Ask, "What does commitment to marketing look like to you?"

More squirming. "I just expected you to really focus on it, you know?"

More clarifying. "What results would you see if I focused on it more?"

You may start getting somewhere now. "I thought you'd spend 20 hours a week on it, at least."

When you get here, you are ready for step two.

2. **Consider It.**

You will want to bristle at this suggestion. You will think, *TWENTY HOURS A WEEK? Is he insane? Does he have any idea how much I have going on right now?!*

I encourage you to say instead, "Well, let me consider that. Twenty hours wasn't what I thought you would say, but let me think on that. Can you tell me why that makes sense to you?"

Stay open. You've made it this far. This is when the conversations turns from an issue that attacks you personally to a true problem to solve—together.

"We need to stay on top of the blog, get events on the calendar every few months, and be better about marketing to our existing clients. There's so many deals that could come from them; they are already loyal!"

Have an honest dialog about what needs to be done and then figure out how it would work for you. Put on your negotiating hat and figure out together what is necessary and what isn't. Be honest about the time you have to commit to those things. It is tempting to overcommit at this juncture but I encourage you to under promise and over deliver. Instead of disappointing them and yourself, you will be given the opportunity to dazzle them with your efforts. Delegate the leftovers or shelve them with a date to revisit them. All outcomes are welcome as long as they are communicated clearly.

3. **Make a Promise.**

Tell him what you heard as the outcome of your dialog. "I commit to ten hours a week for marketing and emailing you a list of completed projects every Friday by noon. Are we on the same page?"

He will agree or disagree. Keep working on the wording until you've got it down and stick to it. If you agreed to do an update on Friday, he can't ask about it on Thursday. Well, he *can*, and then you can say (not growl!) that you will have it to him by Friday noon, as promised. If you committed to work ten hours on marketing, make it happen. If your son gets sick Wednesday and you see that you aren't going to be able to keep your commitment, let him know. Even though he lives in the same house, he does not see the same needs that you do. Communication is key.

Here is the best way (the way that works and builds vs. erodes trust) to communicate when you are not going to keep a promise: "I know we agreed I would have the updates to you by Friday noon, but I need to make a new promise this week. My schedule got significantly changed when I had to stay home with Jimmy, but I plan to catch up this weekend, so my new promise is that I will email you the updates by the end of the day Monday. Will that work?"

Once agreed, then, guess what? You are not breaking your promise or slacking on your commitment when you don't meet the usual Friday noon deadline. You have made a NEW promise, it was agreed upon, and when you fulfill it on Monday, your partnership will still be intact.

This process only works if you trust the other person to follow through. That will erode if you don't hold up your end of the bargain. Promises are meant to be kept and expectations are meant to be set. Yes, life happens and you have to change a promise sometimes, but make that an exception, not a habit, if you want to show up as a reliable partner.

4. **Recognize Accomplishments**

Once the expectations are set, start looking for their successes and recognize them. "Wow, you've really amped up your marketing efforts and I'm seeing a 20% increase in inquiries. Thanks." It doesn't take much to show him that you're thankful for his efforts.

Criticism will still raise its ugly head from time to time. I encourage you to talk about the conditions of satisfaction each time that happens rather than letting it fester and take hold in your heart. Both of you deserve to hear the truth rooted in love, understanding, and acceptance.

Steps to Align Expectations

ARGUMENT SPILLOVER

I walked into the kitchen and my shoes stuck to whatever sugary substance covered the floor. I resigned myself to mopping as I made my way to the fridge, hearing the telltale squeaking of the spill follow me throughout the length of the galley kitchen. "Hey guys, did you spill anything?" I asked my kids who were sitting at the kitchen table.

"Yeah, but I cleaned it up all by myself," my five-year-old answered.

"He dropped the jug of ice tea, Mommy! The corner burst open!" my eight-year-old chimed in, eager to get the facts straight. "It's in the sink."

I looked up at the counter and realized the spill was all over the counter and still dripping onto the floor. The ice tea jug was, indeed, in the sink and resting on top of a syrup-covered plate. I sighed and got to work on the sink, the counter, the cabinets, the jug, and the floor.

My son had certainly tried to clean it up by himself but he had not realized the extent of the mess he had inadvertently caused. He saw only the immediate problem—the spill on the floor.

Arguments are very similar. We can get into an argument and suddenly that problem and feeling of angst flows beyond the initial discussion and into all the crevices of our lives.

Argument spillover can be even more problematic for couples that work together all day. *Spillover* is defined as, "an unexpected consequence, repercussion, or byproduct." While it is unexpected, it is also a familiar enemy. We fight about a parenting decision over breakfast then have to go into a budget meeting at the office. We're still angry that he said "that" and we can't even hear his business topic ideas for what they are. We're just wondering if those voodoo dolls really work and if you could pick one up over lunch. He questions one of your ideas and you shoot back a nasty response. Now he's even madder than he was this morning and it's only 10 AM.

Both of you want to be treated with respect but that's the hardest gift to give in the middle of self-righteous anger. You wait for him to earn back your kindness and he does the same. That loop will not end unless you have a moment to gain some perspective. You need an emotional time-out to gather your thoughts and feelings and then complain to God. But how do you find that time in the midst of a crazy day?

Close the door, mute your phone, and sit down for a few moments of silence. Breathe. Ask the spirit to fill you with forgiveness. "You must forgive one another just as the Lord has forgiven you" (Colossians 3:13). That's a hard one, I know. Sometimes I have to thank God for forgiving me for all the times I've messed up before I'm ready to forgive Dane. I have to reframe it and remember that my feelings are valid and important but they won't be heard if I present them with anger. Once you feel the softness returning to your heart, you are ready to address the conflict.

Make it Happen (10 Minutes)

You cannot avoid conflict; you are married and work together, for goodness sakes. But you do have the option of addressing when and how it will get resolved.

1. **Resolve It Now.**

   Cancel the meeting, close the office door and get it done if the argument is dripping like that jug of iced tea and interfering with productivity. Spending 20 minutes to get to the bottom of it might be just the thing to change the trajectory of your day. Be the first one to approach your partner with forgiveness and kindness and you might just see their anger dissipate before your eyes.

2. **Agree to Shelve It Until a Specific Time.**

   He might be too mad. You might be too busy. You both might be sick of talking in circles. It's okay to reschedule a discussion for a better time. Plan a long lunch far away from the ears of your employees. Schedule a 3:00 coffee break. Agree to talk at 8:30 after the kids are fast asleep. It doesn't matter when or where. It just matters that you make the choice together and keep that promise to each other. You are not allowed to avoid this conversation. Create an appointment or alarm on your phone so that you both know this is a priority. It's unsettling, to say the least, to have the fission of conflict between you. Knowing a resolution is near will give you the ability to truly "shelve it" and move forward with your day.

3. **Let It Go!**

   I cannot hear those words without hearing Elsa from the movie, *Frozen*, singing it loudly and grandly. "Let it Go! Let it Go!" There was liberation in her voice and it can be in yours, too. Sometimes I walk away from a fight and think, "What in the world was that about? That was the silliest thing we've ever fought about!" My favorite was the time we fought about me taking his clothes to the dry cleaner for him. He was upset that I hadn't told them to forgo the pleat in his flat-front pants. I was trying to do a nice thing but instead created an annoying issue for him. We both agreed to just *let it go*. You can too. Not everything has to be dissected, digested, and deliberated. Sometimes you just get mad and say something dumb to each other. Accept it and agree (Agree!!) to both let it go.

RESOLVING CONFLICT

You've agreed to sit down and talk about the conflict but what happens when that door clicks shut? I'll bet you can predict the way the discussion will go because you've been in this seat so many times before. He'll say this and then you'll say that and then he'll get defensive and then you'll present your case with more gusto and end up…nowhere. Let's figure out how to break you out of your normal argument cycle. The Bible gives us a great starting point.

"If your brother or sister sins, go and point out their fault, just between the two of you. If they listen to you, you have won them over. But if they will not listen, take one or two others along, so that every matter may be established by the testimony of two or three witnesses. If they still refuse to listen, tell it to the church; and if they refuse to listen even to the church, treat them as you would a pagan or a tax collector" (Matthew 18:15-17).

This verse was the cornerstone of a session on positive conflict resolution at a marriage conference. We walked into the ballroom and settled in our seats, confident that this would be a breeze.

"We rarely fight," I said smugly.

Dane linked his hand with mine and looked at me with love. "That's true," he said simply.

We sat in our seats and pulled out our workbook to take notes, thinking that we could probably have hosted this particular session. Little did we know that a lesson in humility was awaiting us right outside those doors.

"So, what do you want to do for our date assignment tonight?" I asked Dane as we gathered our things. I had been really looking forward to this; we so rarely had one-on-one time anymore.

"We can go out to dinner or something, then I was planning on meeting James downstairs to watch the hockey game," he said innocently. There were several other couples from our church at this conference and he had apparently been making plans.

I felt my face go red hot and my chest tighten. We were supposed to connect! We were at a *marriage conference* for goodness sakes! I took a deep breath and forged ahead.

"It's supposed to be a date, babe. I wanted time for *us*," I said as I fought with dashed expectations, annoyance, anger, and a deep fear that he didn't want to be with me as much as I wanted to be with him.

"I know. We'll go on our date then you'll go to sleep and I'll watch the game. No big deal," he said, still blissfully unaware of my mounting emotions.

"Get out your notes from the session," I said. "We're going to need them."

We headed up to our hotel room to use every one of our new tools. We spoke awkwardly as we tried to navigate a new way of speaking to each other, measuring each word against new standards. I shared my hurt, he shared his complete confusion about why this was an issue at all. Eventually, he was able to hear me and I was able to hear him. He didn't end up watching that hockey game and I was secure that he was doing it out of love, not guilt or obligation.

We all have disagreements—some petty, some astronomical. We are intrinsically different and we can really drive each other nuts. Combine two people from different backgrounds with different idiosyncrasies and stir in a bit of life's inevitable challenges and it's bound to explode at some point. We can't totally avoid conflict no matter how hard we try to keep the peace.

You and I both have the unique challenge of being married to a man and a business. I have found that my differences become more pronounced at work because "Work Kate" is a very different persona than "Wife Kate." Can you guess which Kate is easier to get along with? Wife Kate goes with the flow and lets Husband Dane lead most things. She is encouraging, patient, and gentle. She is a great listener and works hard to make sure he feels loved and cared for. Business or Work Kate, however, is driven and focused. She is convicted about her ideas and plans and struggles with any interference. She loves a challenge and goes after goals full force. Poor Work Dane.

Make it Happen (15 Minutes)

Conflict has become much more commonplace than it was in the days of the marriage conference. Our lives, business, and family are expanding, so of course there is more and more opportunity for problems to crop up. We differ on things ranging from parenting to client gifts and we are forever thankful for the things we've learned along the way about conflict resolution. We're not great at it—it's so hard to put aside our own agendas and really listen. But we have learned that there are five things that will give you a resolution.

1. **Fighting the Urge to Isolate**

   Anger makes you want to be alone. The last thing you want is to look at that person that made you want to scream ten minutes before. There's a healthy factor to taking a step back. The cerebral cortex of your brain is the center of logic and judgment while your limbic system is responsible for emotional responses. During a flash of anger your amygdala (the home of your "fight or flight" response) hijacks your brain and isolates the response to your limbic, or emotional, system. It takes at least 20 minutes for the cerebral cortex to kick in and override your comments with sound judgment. Twenty minutes! A lot of non-constructive or hurtful things can be said in 20 minutes. It's much wiser to walk away when you are in the throes of anger. Counting to 10, or to 10,000, helps me when I am seeing red.

   The isolation becomes problematic when it extends beyond a few hours. The conflict grows in your mind and assumptions are made. These assumptions only fuel your anger and "build your case." If you are approaching your marriage as a prosecuting attorney does a case, you are not working toward oneness. You are for "I win, you lose." If you are hiding in the brush like a rabbit rather than facing the problem at hand, you are not working toward oneness. You are for "No fight means I can't lose."

I know conflict is scary. I personally have had to do a LOT of work to be able to face anger. It felt so threatening (my anger and others') until a counselor shared something very wise with me. "Kate, anger is God's way of protecting you," she explained. "It is a signal that you have been wronged in some way. It's a flare in the sky that tells you there is an emotional emergency. The trick is to find the underlying problem. How have you been wronged and what does that make you feel once you accept and process the anger?"

She helped me to allow anger to have a role in my life. I learned that I don't have to hide from conflict or give anger so much power. Anger must be understood and respected. It is not something to be used during conflict resolution. Again, a lot of mean things can be said in 20 minutes. But if you feel it or your spouse feels it, there is something deeper that feels violated. Once you are both ready to communicate that feeling, you are ready to confront each other.

2. **Lovingly Confront**

There is an art to confrontation. Timing, tone, and intent all need to line up for a positive result. I learned a long time ago that I can't control all those things and I have to fall on my knees before I have a tough conversation with Dane. I ask God to fill me with wisdom and rid me of my selfishness. I ask him to open both of our hearts and minds so that we can hear each other's hurt and that the pain somehow, some way, draws us closer to God and closer to each other. I find that surrendering this result to Jesus takes the pressure off of me and also reminds me of the purpose of this talk. The purpose is not to prove my point (as much as it pains me!). The purpose is to seek resolution.

Time gives the gift of perspective. When you do sit down to address this issue, remember this wisdom from Proverbs 15:1: "A soft answer turns away wrath, but a harsh word stirs up anger." Know that your spouse may not see their "faults" as clearly as you do. Sit on your hands when you start to feel the need to finger-point. We're all guilty of crossing boundaries when they haven't yet been clearly defined. If you start listing your spouse's faults, the conversation will be shut down. No resolution emerges from a bout of mud wrestling.

It's important that he is in a good place to talk as well. The times that I have brought up a conflict as he was furiously typing an email or just coming out of a tough meeting have blown up in my face. Prepare your heart and then ask God to show you the right time. It's never going to be at the end of a long and trying day. It is almost never going to be his right time at the same moment as when you are ready to talk about it. Oh, the peace that could prevail if only we would stop expecting that! If it's feeling like you are both in a very stressful season and there's never going to be a perfect time, schedule it. I know, I know. You think I'm crazy. But it really helps when the other person knows that there's something pressing on your mind that needs to be resolved. It will give them time to get in the right head space instead of jumping in with an attack of "we need to talk." You are not the only one who may feel the need to pray for an open heart and mind before having a difficult conversation.

Once you are ready to talk, the best way to get started is to pray together. It can feel awkward at first, especially when you are geared up about addressing this really tough issue. I promise it will disarm both of your defensiveness and show that you have a shared goal of working this out. It sets the tone.

3. **One Issue at a Time**

Ever heard of the term, "kitchen sinking"? It happens when you throw all kinds of events, or mistakes, at someone all at once. It looks like this:

"I was really hurt when you cancelled our date night to take that appointment."

"Oh yeah? How do you think I felt when you went out with your friends last week instead of finishing that proposal I needed? You came in late and woke me up. Then you had the nerve to complain about how much money you spent going out with them!"

At this point, you can take the bait or get back on track with the original issue. Their response is inflammatory and it makes you want to jump in and defend yourself. But if you do, the conversation becomes a never-ending rabbit hole of accusations. It leaves your heart broken and your head spinning. It certainly does not lead to a healthy resolution. If another issue comes up, even as an example, interrupt and say, "Wait, we're getting off track. Let's get back to the original issue." If they resist, you may need to reassure them that you are willing to talk about the additional issues with them, but not now, not until the original one is handled.

Focusing your talk gives you both a clear objective to work toward. The problem begins to separate from the person and you begin to work as a team to solve it. For example, if you are upset because you have asked him to stop spending and he hasn't, the discussion may reveal that you need to develop a solid budget. You can both work to find the best way to accomplish that goal and keep each other accountable. The image you do not want is one where you are standing opposite one another, talking *at* each other. The image you do want is where you are standing shoulder-to-shoulder, facing the one issue together, side-by-side… looking *together* for a solution. You are both then focused on the problem, not on each others' shortcomings.

4. **Listen Without Interrupting**

You may be the one who has the issue initially. You may be the one that scheduled the conversation. This does not, however, give you the floor for the entire conversation.

"Be sure you are ready to take it as well as dish it out," says FamilyLife Ministries. "You may start to give your spouse some 'friendly advice' and soon learn that what you are saying is not really his problem, but yours!"

This is a two-way street. You have contributed to this problem in some way, even if it was just lack of communication. My husband likes to say that it's like a football team watching game film. I gave him a completely blank face when he said it the first time and he explained it like this: "They watch the entire game together noting how they could have done things differently. They learn from their mistakes. They learn how to work better as a team."

What do you think would happen if one of the football players shouted out, "But that's not fair! I couldn't catch it because of your throw!" I don't think he'd get any better, do you? Neither can we unless we seek ways to take personal responsibility for what we did, or maybe what we neglected to do. Be open. Be ready to see how you can improve.

Once you have presented the issue in a kind way, i.e., "I am nervous about the amount of money we spend each month," take a little time to elaborate on your feelings. Explain why it makes you uneasy. What are you afraid of happening? How does it affect you when you see the credit card balance?

Notice that there were no "You" statements in this example. "You won't stop spending!" and "You don't even care that we are down to only two months of savings!" will only shut them down. Sharing your feelings introduces vulnerability and opens the door for them to do the same.

Your spouse's job is to repeat those things back to you. "It sounds like my spending is making you worry. You want to have at least six months in the bank to feel secure. Do I have that right?"

They may or may not get it right. Take time to clarify any statements that don't ring true to you until you feel as if they understand your feelings. And then zip your lip and listen. It's their turn.

Fight your urge to defend yourself. You owe your partner an open mind and you just might realize that you are inadvertently contributing to the problem. Maybe you hadn't communicated that you wanted six months of savings in the bank until that moment. How would he know he had overspent if you hadn't told him that important piece of information? Listen with everything you have and repeat what you hear back to him once he has finished sharing his feelings.

Note: Dane was not big on identifying feelings when we first got married. He has said to me, "I didn't even know there were so many feeling words until I met you!"

Maybe one or both of you struggle with that, too. If you do, I have some help to offer. A counselor gave us a list of feeling words for him to try out. He would place each word in this sentence to see if it fit. "I feel _____ when you _____". One would resonate and that was the one he chose to use in our conversations. Again, it was awkward for awhile. Remember learning how to ride a bike? It takes practice to get it right. Today he is thankful to have a solid emotional intelligence that translates into all of his relationships. It's worth it, I promise.

Here's a quick list of negative emotions to give you a starting point.

Frustrated	Jealous
Worried	Angry
Overwhelmed	Annoyed
Afraid	Sad

5. **Agree on Action**

Resolution will happen once you both agree to an action. What is the outcome of your discussion? Are you going to have weekly budget meetings? Are you going to limit spending by using a cash system? Agree on that result and then take it one step further. Decide on an accountability plan. Ask each other, "What should I do if I see this happening again?"

He may just want you to remind him or he may want you to take some kind of action; maybe you would take the credit cards out of their wallet if the spending continues. Listen and follow through. This will give you a feeling of safety because you have a plan moving forward. He will have buy-in because it was his idea.

I can tell you from experience that it's incredibly difficult to break confrontation habits. You both already have a style of fighting and working things out and you will fall back on those as you talk. Prayer and the perfect mindset will go right out the window if you don't stay vigilant throughout the conversation. It's okay to take a five-minute "time out" and resume with calmer energy. It may be a good idea to pray again before resuming the conversation.

During the discussion, sometimes I have to do breath prayers. I breathe in and silently pray, *Lord, fill me with you*, then I will breathe out and say, *rid me of myself.* Sometimes my prayers are less beautiful. *Lord, let me not strangle him*, and then, *give me strength*. God knows your heart—the wording doesn't matter. He always comes through for me and He will for you, too. Stay faithful and stay connected. You and your spouse will become stronger and closer because of this.

6

Keys to Communication

Be gracious in your speech.
The goal is to bring out the best in others
in a conversation, not put them down
not cut them out.

Colossians 4:6 MSG

HOW COMMUNICATION BUILDS TRUST

Ever feel misunderstood? Not heard? Unloved? Communication breakdowns are almost always the root of the problem when we speak to couples. Different communication styles, withheld information or feelings, and the distractions of life seem to hinder every attempt at healthy communication. Withholding or lying, i.e., being secretive, is the carbon monoxide in the room; it is not visible, but it will slowly kill the relationship.

"He promised me he would never start another business," Olivia said during a meeting with me. She poured a cup of coffee for each of us and circled around her kitchen island to replace the pot, mentally preparing to share one of the darkest periods of her marriage.

"Did you know we've been married 30 years? Thirty years…I still can't believe it. We almost didn't make it, Kate."

The story began to pour out. She shared that their early marriage was nearly destroyed by a failed business venture. She had been supportive as a young wife and helped handle the bookkeeping for the business. She worked another job to provide them with health insurance and other benefits but after the birth of their first child, it became too much. She stepped back from their business.

"I decided to keep my job to keep the benefits but have more time to focus on our son," she said. The recession hit and their business began to hemorrhage money, but her husband kept that from her. No longer having a hands-on role, Olivia trusted her husband to keep her abreast of what was going on in the business, but there was no particular structure for that in place. "I just kept thinking the money from the next job would pay for the losses," he said. "I figured I didn't need to tell her because I had it handled. But I didn't."

He shared how much pressure he felt as the sole provider. He couldn't imagine letting her down, so he continued to live on false hope, incurring more and more debt. Eventually, he realized they were facing bankruptcy and the only option was to tell her the truth.

"I still remember that day. Do you?" Olivia asked her husband.

He had been mostly quiet until then, taking his lumps, as they say. He folded his hands in his lap and looked at them intently, avoiding eye contact. "Yep. We took a walk and I told you."

She leaned forward, her eyes still filled with the pain of the memory. "I was devastated, Kate. Devastated. Not about the money but about the lying. I made him promise to get a job and never buy another business."

He laughed then and said, "But that didn't exactly happen, did it?"

"No, it didn't. But that's because you run this one differently."

They are now on their third business and this one is successful and healthy. I asked them what changed and he said it beautifully: "God is the CEO of this one."

"And we don't have any secrets from each other," she said.

He nodded in agreement and said, "No secrets."

As that couple learned, secrets (withheld information or feelings) are toxic. They cause the death of good communication and can lead to the demise of a marriage and business. This couple learned the hard way that avoiding tough discussions only creates division, and the breakdown in communication became an obstacle that was almost insurmountable. The breakdown in trust took years of work with a couples' therapist to repair and restore.

We find a million reasons to justify our silence. "He is already stressed out enough, so I'm really protecting him by keeping this to myself." Being a martyr may have short-term pay-offs but never contributes to the health of a relationship. Then there is the justification that "I have to remain focused and strong enough to fix this, so I better not subject myself to her wrath and punishment I'm sure to receive if she found out." This is cowardice and only puts off facing the problem, and asking for your partner's help to find a solution.

Trusting our partner, and feeling certain that our partner trusts us, is of utmost importance. Communicating in an honest, healthy way is the best way to build and maintain trust.

Communication is the core of a relationship. It's the oxygen a marriage and business partnership must have to breathe and thrive. The definition of communication is simple: the exchange of ideas or information. However, the brain activity during communication is so complicated it boggles the mind.

"When you communicate face-to-face with your spouse, your message is made up of three parts: content, which is only 7 percent; tone of voice, which is 38 percent; and nonverbal communication, which is 55 percent," writes Dr. H. Norman Wright, author of *Communication: Key to Your Marriage.*

Your Message

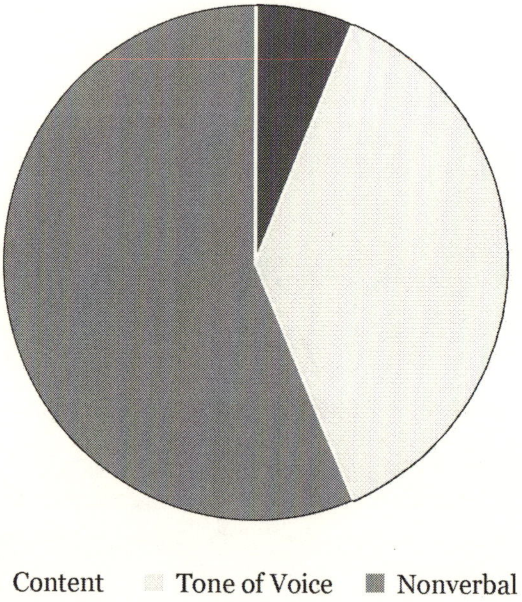

Our interpretation of those three elements is impacted greatly by our frame of mind (internal noise/mind chatter), our history (including emotional baggage), and the current situation. As we all know from experience, timing is everything. Sometimes, I can receive a communication from my husband without feeling defensive, impatient, or irritated, yet other times the exact same communication attempt would trigger my "less than open" side.

For example, if your computer just went on the fritz, you are not going to be open to your husband telling you about the latest cloud back-up software. You'd be too upset about not backing up your data and might retort with something like, "Well that would have been helpful to know YESTERDAY!"

Every relationship has communication challenges. With your partner, these challenges must not only be met day by day; it is imperative to "get to the bottom of it." If your well water is clouded with some dark grey particles, it is useful to filter the water before drinking it. But even more importantly, the source of the contamination must be discovered and remedied. This frees up so much time and energy that had been necessary to spend on filtering. Going to the source and resolving the issue is always the best approach.

A business owner I know decided to purchase a postage metering machine for the office and he swears it saved his marriage. He and his wife had arguments at least once or twice month about who did or did not make a trip to the post office, handle the outgoing mail in a timely manner, or keep on hand an adequate supply of stamps. One day the argument started to sound just too familiar and he finally asked himself, "What is missing here? What would resolve this once, and for all?" The answer came to him immediately, and their partnership became free of postage bickering.

Both arguing and avoiding arguing by withholding are examples of communication being choked off, leaving the relationship without oxygen, without the ability to breathe and thrive. But what about the messages that are hiding under the surface?

Much, much more mass of an iceberg lies under the surface than what is visible to us as we approach it from on top of the water. Communication is like that. Previously, I quoted Dr. Wright who wrote a book about communication. "Content…is only seven percent; tone of voice…is 38 percent; and nonverbal communication…is 55 percent." In other words, the words you hear coming out of the other person's mouth are only the tip of the iceberg! Real communication cannot occur if you do not do what is necessary to hear what is under the surface; thus, you must develop your own listening skills that are as effective as sonar.

Good communication and partnership are inseparable. Do you remember when you were first married and you started getting used to saying things like, "We should invite the Smiths over for dinner," or "We need to get a new dryer"? More and more, you and your spouse started using "we" instead of "I" as your marriage bond strengthened and your partnership grew. The Bible acknowledges this process of "two" becoming "one" in many places, including the following: Genesis 2:24: "Therefore a man shall leave his father and his mother and hold fast to his wife, and they shall become one flesh."

Ecclesiastes 4:9: "Two are better than one, because they have a good return for their labor: If either of them falls down, one can help the other up. But pity anyone who falls and has no one to help them up. Also, if two lie down together, they will keep warm. But how can one keep warm alone?"

"We" is an entity with needs that surpass your own. That means that you won't always get what you want. That means no secrets, even when it's embarrassing or shameful. That means that your partner's happiness and success is as important to you as your own. Live with the relationship's needs at the forefront.

Remember, communication is about exchanging ideas, not badgering someone until they see things your way. The goal is to work toward unity, not power. Shed your selfishness. What is best for both of you? It may take some compromising. That vacation you've been wanting may be on the backburner for six months due to other priorities he is right to point out, but it still has a place on the calendar.

Without a strong sense of "we," good communication becomes a struggle, nearly impossible. Without good communication, having confidence that "we" can handle anything, together, becomes nearly impossible. Partnership and communication are interdependent. If you feel that one of them is suffering, face both and give each your best effort. The connection is there—when one is improved, the other area will benefit as well.

Make it Happen (20 Minutes)

1. **Be Aware**

   What internal and external noises are in your life at this moment? Is that impacting your reaction? If so, take an emotional inventory and figure out what is really bothering you. You may have thought that you were sick of the dishes stacking up when it's really that you are feeling overwhelmed with the amount of responsibilities that fall on your shoulders.

2. **Make Three Lists:**

   One, a list of reoccurring arguments, big or small. Don't take time to assign blame or imagine solutions right now, just write everything down.

Two, make a list of reoccurring complaints you have, big or small. You will find things for this list that are not on the previous account of arguments, because you haven't communicated them. In fact, precisely to avoid an argument, you've kept some complaints to yourself, some which have begun to fester resentment. Write all these down.

Your third list is for everything you can think of that your spouse complains about to you, or that you perceive is their complaint with you, even if not verbalized.

3. **Pray Over Your Lists**

   Once you have your three lists, put them aside. Don't discuss them with your spouse until you've "slept on it" and prayed about it. Choosing what is important to communicate from your newfound awareness is a big responsibility. Again, sleep on it and pray about it first.

4. **Talk It Over**

   Ideally, your partner will make their own corresponding lists. Then you will not only become extraordinarily more aware of your own issues, but in sharing, you both will gain valuable perspective as you learn about each other.

   Take responsibility for how this discussion will go. Be aware of your body language. Relax your shoulders, soften your expression and sit near him or even hold his hand as you speak. There is great power in touch. Ask how you can be a better partner and be open to the things he has to say. Your tone should be encouraging as you each work to help each other grow into better people and a stronger couple.

LISTENING VS. UNDERSTANDING

There's a video online (YouTube), "It's Not About the Nail." The first time I saw it I laughed and was impressed that someone had taken the time to make such a creative video to make a point that so many people would be able to relate to. A couple is seated on a couch and the woman has a large nail jutting from her forehead. Yes, a nail, which looks like it has been stuck partway into her head (don't worry, there is no blood, it's not that kind of video).

She is not crying, but is distraught. She is complaining to the man about her nagging headaches. He tries to "fix it" by telling her to just take out the nail. She ignores his suggestion as if there is no nail. She tries a different tactic of explaining the impact the headache is having on her life but he continues to suggest she simply take out the nail, or let him do it. After the third or fourth time, she gets frustrated and shouts, "It's not about the nail!"

How often do we do that to our spouses when they are telling us about something that is going on with them? We see the solution so clearly and think that they just need to take the right advice and the problem will disappear. While that may be the case, most people need to work through a problem in their own way and in their own time.

Men and women feel heard in contrasting ways. Women need confirmation as we speak. Our girlfriends will say things like, "I totally get it," or "That is completely normal!" Recently my friend said, "Been there, done that." In four words, she assured me that I was not experiencing something uniquely personal, that in fact she had been through the same thing and here she is… living proof she got through it and I can too. We tend to use these well-meaning interjections with our husbands, too, but what they usually need is quite different.

There is a reason that a book about this very topic has sold over 50 million copies. Being unaware of these differences leads to failed relationships. *Men Are from Mars, Women Are from Venus* is a book written by American author and relationship counselor John Gray. The book states that most common relationship problems between men and women are a result of fundamental psychological differences between the sexes, which the author exemplifies by means of the metaphor that men and women are from different planets, and that each sex is acclimated to its own planet's society and customs, but not to those of the other. One example is men's complaints that if they offer solutions to problems that women bring up in conversation, the women are not necessarily interested in solving those problems, but mainly want to talk about them. Gray asserts each sex can be understood in terms of distinct ways they respond to stress and stressful situations, and really in every aspect of communication.

As I said, women give and receive validating statements during a conversation, but this is not typical for men. What I have learned is that my husband needs to have a quiet listener in order to feel heard.

Simply maintaining eye contact and an open posture will lead him to say, "Wow, thanks for listening without interrupting my train of thought. That helped."

The more certain you are that you have the "right answer," the less helpful you may be. Being a good listener means that you don't jump in with your right answer until you have asked enough questions and listened enough to actually understand *why* they have not already come up with the answer you are anxious to provide. On the other hand, if you just love being "right," you will throw your answer out like a life preserver with no tether and say "grab this or sink" as you walk away. If they don't grab it and they sink, well... you told them! See, you were right?

Being right holds no rich rewards like being in a loving partnership with your spouse does. I know what your priority is, what your values mean to you...or you wouldn't be reading this book. Listening, understanding, and communicating are learnable skills. I'm teaching you how to practice them. I want you to fully engage in these distinctions and written exercises, and by doing so, you can save your business and your marriage.

"Mom and I were competitive," my father said of his business and life partner. "I would interfere even though she was running the company. I would tell her my ideas. I was critical and that would tap into her insecurities. She would say things like, 'You are questioning me! You don't believe in me!' We even named the interaction, 'The Loop of Terribleness.'"

Are you caught in the "Loop of Terribleness"? It will not be rectified until you put down your sword and shield and seek to understand. Remember, marriage is about coming together, not being right (I know, I know. It's not as fun. But it works better, I promise). So what does it mean to not just listen but *understand*? I love this definition: "*Understanding* (recognition) combines hearing and listening. It implies taking of proper action by comprehending what was heard."

1. **Seek to Understand**

"You have to seek to understand before you seek to be understood," my mom would say each time I brought her a conflict. She knew to bring this admonition out whenever I was feeling particularly self-righteous. I never wanted to hear it because I already had my argument so carefully crafted. I was sure that if I just had a chance to lay out the "facts," the opposing party (usually my sister) would most certainly see how wrong she had been. If I chose to ignore Mom's advice, the argument would only escalate. If I chose to put my agenda aside and seek first to understand, my eyes would be opened to another perspective and my "facts" would tend to fall flat. My mom was gently reminding me to admit my fault rather than defend it. She was teaching me to reach out in love and understanding. The prayer of St. Francis includes:

O, divine master grant that I may
not so much seek to be consoled as to console,
to be understood as to understand.

Dane and I had to institute a habit of saying, "That sounds really difficult. Are you coming to me for advice or would you rather I just listen?" It has changed things immensely. We found that we listen to each other better when our subconscious isn't busy trying to solve the problem. We focus on the emotion of the other person and spend our brain power trying to give them comfort. The truth is that we almost always have a solution already in mind. We just don't like the process of having to deal with the problem at all. Once the complaining is off our chest, we're ready to take on the problem full force.

2. **Build Their Emotional Bank Account**

Our family went to therapy when I was a teenager and I learned something invaluable in one of those sessions. The therapist introduced the theory of an emotional bank account. "Every time someone does something kind for you, like saying something encouraging, they make a deposit into your emotional bank account. If they yell or make a cutting remark or lie, they make a withdrawal. Healthy relationships are constantly making deposits and sometimes making withdrawals. Unhealthy relationships have overdrawn bank accounts." Very clear, right?

The Bible is clear on this one as well. "Sitting down, Jesus called the Twelve and said, "Anyone who wants to be first must be the very last, and the servant of all" (Mark 9:35).

We are called by Christ to be a servant of all; to make deposits into other peoples' emotional bank accounts on a consistent basis. The crazy thing is that we all expect deposits to come in different forms. Gary Chapman discusses this phenomenon in his book, *The 5 Love Languages*. Chapman asserts that you may give or receive love in any of these languages: Acts of Service, Words of Affirmation, Quality Time, Receiving Gifts, or Physical Touch. Your partner's primary love language may not match yours and it takes extra effort to communicate your love in a way they can receive it. There is an online quiz you can take to find out your primary love languages and it is eye-opening to say the least.

I discovered that I need words of affirmation to feel loved, while Dane's giving love language is gifts. He would bring something home for me once a week. He brought flowers, t-shirts from places he had traveled, a new pair of shoes I had mentioned that I liked. I thought it was all very sweet (especially since the shoes were actually cute) but I wanted more. I couldn't pin point why all those loving gestures weren't speaking to me. The Love Language test revealed the answer. I needed him to *say* things, not *buy* things. I needed to hear that he thinks I'm the best mom in the world, that I'm beautiful, that he loves the room I redecorated, that he was impressed by my patience with that difficult client. It's not natural to him, but he makes a major effort to do that for me.

His love language is quality time. He wants to be with me even if we're not interacting. He likes to know I am there. I, however, had spent all my time giving him words of affirmation. (Since these were so important to me, I gave him what I thought was a wonderful way to show my love.) He wasn't feeling as if he was a priority to me because I wasn't speaking his language. See the power in this?! (By the way, knowing the primary love language of each of your children can be very useful, too. One may respond to getting a bear hug while another feels special when you spend extra time making a teddy bear cake together.)

Make it Happen (10 Minutes)

Take ten minutes to take your love language test on www.5lovelanguages.com. Have your spouse do the same, then sit down to fill out this diagram and talk about how this might change how you communicate love and respect to each other. How can you begin to incorporate their primary love language into your interactions?

Love Languages

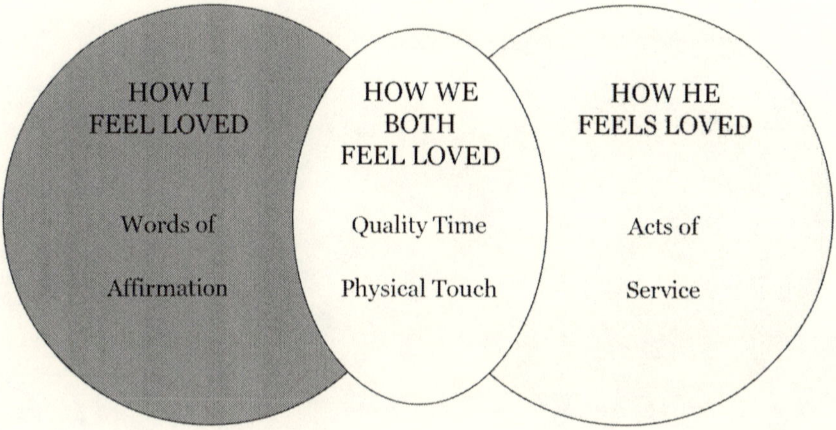

Diagram 6.0

7

A New Kind of Commitment

I can do all things through Him
who strengthens me.

Phillipians 4:13 NIV

We each have different decision-making personalities and these differences can create tension and even serious relationship issues. There are two specific types: decisive and thorough. *Decisive* decision makers gather information and "know" the right thing to do. They make decisions based on their gut and do not spend much time mulling over the "what-ifs." Once the decision is made, they roll with it. *Thorough* decision makers, however, are analytical, logical, and think about every possible repercussion of each choice. They have spreadsheets, research to back up their spreadsheets, and they do not have much trust in this thing called *intuition*. They cannot be rushed by the decisive decision maker and if they are, mistrust can grow.

Both are necessary in a good partnership. When God created Eve, he told Adam, "I will make a helper suitable for him" (Genesis 2:18). The term "helper" is an honor; in fact God refers to Himself as a helper in Psalm 124:8. Our skills and abilities are designed to naturally complement each other. God made one of you a dreamer and one of you practical for a reason. "You are altogether beautiful, my darling; there is no flaw in you," Solomon shares in Song of Songs 4:7. We need our differences to balance each other out. I am almost always a dreamer but I have found times when I shift to practical. These are usually times when he is dreaming. He's got that part handled so I automatically move to the details of making it happen. That's fantastic as long as we know where the other person falls in the lifecycle of the decision. It's vital to have tools that clarify those steps for you.

If one of you is a *Ready, Fire, Aim* kind of person, you need your partner to slow down the process. If one of you are buried in research and unable to make a decision, you need the decisive one to dig you out of that hole and call it. But we don't always see it that way when we're in the middle of a major decision.

Dane is thorough and practical. I am decisive. We recently redecorated the office and I picked the colors in five minutes. He spent three days choosing a bookshelf, including two trips to the store and several rounds with a measuring tape.

We face the same challenges on major business decisions. My publisher, Barbara Dee, gave us a book called *Built to Sell*. It sat on our coffee table for a few weeks and I picked it up one rainy Saturday afternoon. I read during the entire afternoon, even attempting to fold the laundry while holding the pages of the book open with the laundry basket (don't try it); I couldn't put it down! It was the answer to exactly what we had been seeking—a new recurring revenue stream.

We learned all about a structured program that takes companies through the eight drivers of business value. It starts with an assessment that provides a score and company value, and then outlines specific steps for the business to increase its value over the course of one year. I could see perfectly how we could use this program to prepare potential business brokerage clients for a quick sale and a higher return. It would provide monthly income to us and help expedite the sale of their business when they were ready to pull the trigger.

I kept yelling out things like, "Yes!" and "Dane! This is an answered prayer!" as I read. He would look up from the baseball game and placate me with a smile. I jumped up after the last chapter ready to launch a new consulting business.

"Babe! We can totally use this program! You have to read this. It's the solution we've been asking for!"

He wasn't exactly thrilled. "Consulting is phase two," he said as he got off the couch to grab a beer out the fridge. "We've talked about that. I'm not ready to start consulting yet."

I did know that. But I had no idea when "phase two" would be enacted. No time like the present, right?! I pushed him further and he reluctantly pulled out his laptop. He opened up the website and read it for five seconds then signed up for more information on the Value Builder program.

> "So, what's next?" I asked him, enthusiasm sparkling in my eyes. I was met with a deadpan face.
>
> "I talk to these guys."
>
> "Then what?"
>
> "We'll see if it works for us."

Get out the tape measure...we were in it for the long haul. I brought it up weekly (maybe more if I'm honest). I asked him if he'd spoken to the company. I asked if he'd thought about it more. I again asked him if he had talked with them yet. Finally, he had had it with me.

"You've got to stop! I told you I would look into it and I will. I am not even ready to do this and you won't let it go!"

Ouch. I looked a little deeper to figure out what was going on with me. I wrote about my frustration in my journal and realized I had not been honest with him. "Honey, I'm scared. I'm scared that we start at zero every month. I'm trying to find a way to ensure that money is coming in every month without us working our fingers to the bone. I trust that you will do what you said. I will stop bringing it up," I shared with him one evening.

I prayed for God to help me trust my husband to follow through, and then realized I still wasn't surrendering. *Lord, help me get what I want—and right now!* is not exactly letting go and letting God, is it? I shifted my trust to God and asked Him to make this happen if it was His will. That week, my husband spoke to a Value Builder rep. It was less expensive than we thought and the program provided a huge range of marketing tools. Dane was sold and I felt thankful for the confirmation that this was the right path for us.

There are so many things we could have done better in this process. First, we had not discussed or agreed on when "phase two" would begin. Second, we had completely different goals. I was excited about opening up a recurring revenue stream while he was focused on adding new listings to the brokerage firm. Third, I nagged him to death because we didn't have any kind of deadline. "I will do it" is not a good promise, in terms of communication. There must be a *by when*. The issue hung over our marriage for a month and created anxiety and mistrust. I examined it further and realized that he thought we were having a **conversation for possibilities** and I thought it was a **conversation for results**.

Conversations for possibilities allow both parties to talk openly about what is possible. No idea is a bad idea. It's a dream session. "How about this?" and "How about this?" Conversations for results, however, are designed to execute a decision. A decision is made to commit to one option. It's a go—now let's decide who will do what by when. Very different conversations, right? Both are necessary in the lifecycle of a plan, but if the stage is not defined, communication gets murky and rife with conflict.

Make it Happen (45 Minutes)

Remember using storyboarding to build your family philosophy? This time we are going to leverage that tool to make a decision. Each major decision will involve two sessions: A Possibility Session and Results Session. This exercise works very well whether you and your spouse use it for your decision-making or if the topic indicates others should be involved—employees, partners, or children—if their input is relevant. I am going to use the Value Builder decision Dane and I processed as the framework of the following example storyboard.

POSSIBILITY SESSION

Gather up your supplies to get started. You will need multi-colored sticky notes, scented markers (Crayola and Mr. Sketch both make them), something to play with (stress ball, fidget spinner, a rock garden, slinky… get creative here), and a light snack and water. You want your ideas to address all the senses and this subconsciously helps your brain to think beyond the normal linear ideas.

The organizer places a large card or sticky note across the top with the board's purpose. This clarifies the goal for everyone involved. We chose, "Identify Recurring Revenue Possibilities." Next, create header cards on sticky notes and stick them horizontally across the top of the foam board. These serve as items you want to brainstorm. They will change for every decision. If you get stumped, simply ask yourself what you need to know to make a good decision. What questions do you have? Use those questions as your jumping-off point. I usually start with something that is already in place so that I have a complete visual of "before and after." For example, we started with "Current Revenue Streams" as a starter card. This helps warm up our thinking in an area where we are already comfortable. You can then lead the conversation into thinking beyond the current situation.

Here are some cards from our Recurring Revenue brainstorm.

- Current Revenue Streams
- Recurring Revenue Possibilities
- Programs/Books/Consultants
- Training Options
- A is A: These are the obstacles you have to overcome to make your decision happen. This is a perfect place for all the "that will never work because..." thoughts. This frees up your thinking to move beyond that problem and onto more possibilities. Examples may be, "Cash flow will slow when we shift to recurring revenue model" or "Need staff to handle new product line." Every board needs this card!

Next, open up the session to your spouse and anyone else who may have valuable insights. Give each person a sticky note stack and a marker (and, hopefully, a cookie), and tackle one category at a time. The organizer announces the category and poses it as a question. Start with something silly. We ask questions like, "What are some NFL teams?" or "What are some dog breeds?" Shout out answers for a minute or two. Afterward, everyone's brain will be primed for the task at hand.

Move on to the real reason you are there by addressing the first card and posing a question. For example, "What are our current revenue streams?" Participants yell out their answer as they write them then pass the card to the organizer to stick under that column. I love this part because people get very competitive about getting their answer up first. It energizes their thinking. Encourage them to stretch the boundaries of possibility. There are no bad ideas! You may need to remind the participants of that so no one shoots down another's idea. Coach people to use "yes, and" rather than "no, but." Be sure everyone stays engaged.

If people struggle with answers, the organizer can decide to ask more questions to prompt their thinking. "Are we paid for anything beyond the initial sale?" or "What are our current product lines?" Once the organizer is satisfied, they can move to the next category.

Sometimes the answers people give will fall into a different category. No problem—just stick that card under the appropriate one and keep moving. Remember, no discussion! Keep it fast-paced.

Thank everyone at the end of the session. You will be amazed at all the ideas, but don't let them off the hook yet. It's time to assign some research on any items that need more detail. Ask for volunteers and write the person's initials on the corner of each card he or she commits to research. For example, I needed to look deeper into the specific consulting programs and find out cost, training resources, and marketing options for each of them. Generally, people will volunteer to look into their own ideas and that's fine. Just make sure they are all assigned out.

Set a deadline for their research to be delivered to you. It should be at least a few days before the follow up Results Session. You can set up meetings to discuss their findings or ask for a complete report. Remind them that you are not asking for their opinion, you are asking for facts that will inform your decision. If you and your spouse have agreed to make this decision together, schedule time to pour over the findings. A piece of advice on this one: I encourage you to give one person 51% of the vote. We usually base it on who is going to have to do the lion's share of the implementation of that project and/or decision. If it falls in his wheelhouse, I want to give my input but would rather he make the final call. You may even decide to completely step out of a particular decision. That's fine, too. The exercise not only provides the decision-maker with others' ideas, it stimulates their own thinking in a much more powerful way than if they simply sat down by themselves and noted their thoughts.

Finally, set a date for the Results Session. Your team will want to know what decision you have made and this will give all of you a clear plan for the future. Even if the team consists only of the two of you, the Results Session gives urgency to a decision that may have been floating in and out of conversation for months…or years.

RESULTS SESSION

Pull the card(s) that you have decided to pursue from the Possibilities board and place them on a fresh board. This will give the participants a clear understanding of the direction the company is going to take.

Next, you will need to create a new set of header cards. The goal of this session is to get this decision off the ground. You'll need to define and agree on roles, record the steps to execute the plan, and address potential roadblocks at the start. Here are some sample cards:

- Training Needed
- Marketing
- New Responsibilities
- Processes to Define
- Set-Up Tasks (New forms? Item numbers in accounting system?)
- Costs (Include training, marketing, staff & infrastructure costs)
- Roadblocks (A is A)
- Revenue Expectations

Many of these things will have been uncovered in your research and you may be tempted to skip over something. Please don't! This step will uncover all the to-do's that accompany a major decision. If the entire team isn't aware of all the steps, things will get missed. There's a reason they say "two heads are better than one." The others will think of things you haven't and they are invested in making this a success. Let them be heard.

The same rules apply: No criticism and no discussion. Keep the ideas and insights flowing until you feel that you have a thorough understanding of what needs to be done. Here's an example of the beginnings of a Results Session storyboard.

Give each person an opportunity to volunteer for tasks. I may, for example, volunteer to attend Value Builder training. If I accept that task as my own, I have two options: I can give myself a deadline on the spot or I can commit to a date when I will set the deadline. Sounds a bit crazy, I know. Stick with me. Let's say I don't know when Value Builder holds training sessions. I can't commit to a date to attend yet, can I? I can commit that I will have a date by the end of the week so that I have a chance to find out the details. Always end up with a "by when" or "by when I'll know the by when." Got it? Good.

I will need to update the actual deadline to completing the task (VB Training) on the sticky note as soon as I know the training date. This will give the organizer a complete timeline and a clear expectation of when this will launch. I like to make a master Word document that lists every task chronologically and send it out to my team. This adds another level of accountability and is a great form for me to work from at our weekly meetings. Anything like this that facilitates communication within the team is a great idea.

Here's a quick review of the Results Session steps:

1. Choose a specific goal from the Possibilities Session
2. Write header cards
3. Brainstorm tasks associated with each header card
4. Assign out tasks with deadlines
5. Communicate those deadlines with your team and hold them accountable

We all want to be a valuable part of the team. If your exercise is with just you and your spouse, remember that both of you have incredible talents and insights, but you won't get anywhere if you are like two deer locking horns. I challenge you to take a decision you have been considering and do a practice storyboard session. It can be a decision at home (what smart TV should we buy?) or a work decision (you know, that one you keep talking about in circles). Make it fun! Encourage each other's great ideas and delight in your differences.

When the session is complete, talk about how you can use this to help make other major decisions in your family and at work. Make a list of a few things you'd like to tackle this year and pick one that sounds doable to both of you. Schedule the next session and then sit back and be thankful that God gave you the gift of a life and business partner all in one.

A NEW KIND OF COMMITMENT

We expect deadlines to be set in business. Our employees thrive when they know what is expected of them. And yet that rarely happens in a marriage. We prioritize things automatically without communicating that to the other person. We expect them to "get" that completing a task is important to us. Sometimes we take it even further. Sometimes we think that if they really loved us, they would make it a priority. Ever been there? I know I have.

Dane and I were shopping at Hobby Lobby for "man art" (as he put it). There was a sign that said, "If I tell you I'll do something, I'll do it. You don't have to remind me every six months." We laughed at the truth of that quote.

If I ask Dane to put a bin in the attic, I mean that I want it out of my house right now. He already has a plan for his day (or maybe his whole week) and so he decides to do that chore over the weekend. But he doesn't tell me his plan or his mental deadline. Every day that passes irritates me more. I pass by that bin and feel my annoyance rising and take every opportunity to remind him of this task he said he would do for me. By the weekend, he's had enough of my nagging and I've had enough of his procrastinating. We erupt into an argument. Sound familiar?

Let's unpack this interaction for a minute. We made two specific assumptions:

- Timeline: NOW vs. the weekend
- Priority: 1 vs. 10

Even worse? The trust between us began to erode. "If you assess someone to be sincere, capable, and reliable, then you have trust in them. When you realize you do not trust someone, or someone does not trust you, you should examine these three assessments to discover where the breakdown lies," states Activ8, a leader in communication training.

I trusted that Dane was *sincere* when he committed to getting that bin in the attic. I knew that he wanted to take care of that for me and had every intention of getting it done. I also knew he was *capable* of lifting the bin and placing it in the attic. He had the strength to lift it and the time to execute the task. I did not, however, believe he was *reliable*. Day after day passed and he didn't complete the job. I began to believe that I couldn't count on him when I asked him to do something for me.

Make it Happen (5 Minutes)

We learned to use a step-by-step process of committing to a task and it has revolutionized our interactions. It seems like a lot of components at first, but after a bit of practice it becomes second nature.

1. **Preparation**

   Explain what you need to have done and ask when they would be able to commit to doing it. For example, "I need you to put this bin in the attic. Can you commit to getting this done by Saturday at 5:00 PM?"

2. **Negotiation**

   He has four options at this point:

   - Yes: This means he has agreed and will get it done before or by 5, Saturday.
   - No: He is not willing to complete that task. As hard as this is to hear, he does have the right to say no to whatever you have asked.

- Yes with a different deadline: "I can't do it Saturday because of the golf event but I can commit to getting it done by Sunday at 2."
- Commit to Commit: "I have to check my calendar but I'll get back to you by tonight with a deadline."

Note: This can repeat itself if something changes. The moment he knows he won't be able to make the deadline, he's responsible for letting you know. It might look like this. "I have to help out at the church Sunday so I'm going to need to push back my promise to take the bin to the attic until Monday night." This builds trust between you and shows that the task is a priority.

3. **Performance:** Simply put, get the job done.

4. **Checking back:** He would then come to me and make sure the job has been done to my satisfaction. Maybe he grabbed the wrong bin, or I forgot to tell him there were two bins instead of one. This helps eliminate that communication pitfall.

5. **Acceptance:** Once it's done, thank him for a job well done.

8

Letting Go

The LORD will fight for you; you need only to be still.

Exodus 14:14

DISCOVERING EACH OF YOUR STRENGTHS

My parents gave out pins to each of their new employees that read, "That's the way we've always done it." The words were crossed out in a bold red line.

They had a dynamic and growing software company and wanted innovation to be at the forefront of their employees' minds.

Just because you've always done certain things does not necessarily mean that they are your God-given strengths. In fact, the opposite may be true. But we often don't question our roles. We simply do them because *that's the way you've always done it*. I challenge you to think differently. Change and innovation can be fantastic for your business, your life, and yourself. Even if it is more comfortable to keep the status quo, if things don't make sense, they need to change.

Early in our marriage, it was my job to handle all the bills. I had lived on my own for almost ten years and figured I knew how to handle a checkbook. Except that suddenly, two of us were spending money out of the same account (gasp!). The mental accounting I was used to getting away with (*I spent five bucks at Starbucks and 20 bucks on gas, so we should be good*) wasn't exactly cutting it. We bounced checks and missed payments, but it remained my responsibility.

Fast forward five years and I was still handling our money. I was better at it but not great. There were breakdowns. One time, my sweet husband offered to get up with our newborn son and let me sleep for awhile. He tried to turn on the faucet to run water and warm up milk for my son's bottle. No water. Imagine that…the water gets shut off if you don't pay your bill. The baby started screaming and my husband had to wake me out of my newborn-induced coma to feed the baby. The worst part? This was the third time it had happened and we had thousands of dollars in the bank.

Why, oh why, did I continue to handle the money when it obviously was not one of my strengths? My husband is detail oriented, deadline driven, and very organized. When he packs a suitcase it looks like a display at Gap. When I pack a suitcase, it looks like my closet vomited into it. Optimal money management requires great organization skills, of course. All the signs pointed to Dane being the best one for the job, but neither of us had picked up on it.

Once he took over paying the bills, the water always stayed on and the late notices never showed their mad little faces again. We are both so much more content. I trust he'll get it done and I get to do budgeting, which I enjoy. It only took us half of our marriage to figure it out!

We get comfortable in a certain role and continue doing it because, "that's the way we've always done it." We struggle to get better at things that aren't natural for us. We push ourselves to do things because if we don't do it, who will? I know that this attitude has given me nothing but frustration at myself and my weaknesses. I want more for you.

Did you know that many believe Albert Einstein's wife helped him develop his famous equation after many of his failed attempts? He was a dreamer and lacked focus. His wife was the key to helping him pull his head out of the clouds and obtain success. Have faith that many of your skills will be complementary to your spouse's once they are discovered and documented.

I encourage you to think beyond the roles you have filled at work and at home and approach this with a fresh perspective. Ephesians 2:10 says, "For we are God's handiwork, created in Christ Jesus to do good works, which God prepared in advance for us to do."

When God designed you, He had a very clear purpose for you. He gave you all the aptitude and strengths you need to do God's work. Isn't that amazing? Let's take a moment to pray and prepare your heart.

Dear God,

Thank you for giving me the perfect skill-set to do your work. You designed me with your purposes in mind and I want everything I do to glorify you. Reveal that purpose to me, Lord. Uncover the possibilities. Show me how to use my strengths to grow my marriage, my business, my faith and your kingdom.

In Jesus' name, Amen.

Make it Happen (30 Minutes)

Get your pen and paper out. It's time to get to work. I have a list of questions for you to explore. Take your time with this. If you are stuck, stop and listen for what God has to say to your spirit. He will lead you.

- What personality traits have led to your success?

  Are you outgoing? Determined? Compassionate? Think through some major business wins and explore how your personality impacted that result. For example, "I am creative. This has allowed me to develop innovative marketing campaigns that lead to qualified inquiries and sales." "I am quiet. When I am in a meeting, I listen and take excellent notes that help us in our follow-up." List out as many as you can.

- What do people always tell you that you are great at doing?

  Compliments tend to hold a special place within us. Have you been given the same compliments over time? More accurately, what are you consistently acknowledged for? (You may be complimented on your beautiful smile, but are acknowledged for your ability to stay focused on results.) Are you recognized often for your sales ability or organizational skills? Do people revere your patience or possibly your persistence? List these out.

Note: We often focus more on negative comments than positive ones. If you are struggling with this one, go through your day listening for compliments and acknowledgements. You probably receive them more than you realize. Change your filter to allow positive comments to flow through!

- Ask three people closest to you what your strengths are.

  My friend once gave me a picture that says, "I love you as much as I love coffee." Both of us live on good coffee and it's a sweet and true testament of the gift of our friendship. Your spouse and your best friends love you that much, too. I challenge you to be vulnerable enough to ask them how they see you. They will see you differently than you see yourself and provide valuable insights. Take note of them and feel thankful for their love. "What do you see as my top strengths?" or "What do I do better than most anyone you know?"

- What do you love to do? You know...what are you doing when you are so happily engaged that you lose track of time?

  Hobbies are a portal into your personality strengths. What do you love to do in your free time? Once you've identified a few, think through the personality traits that they require. Do your hobbies involve precision and detail or are they creative and free? Do they reveal your adventurous side or your contemplative one?

- Imagine a project – What role would you fill?

Let's pretend you have to complete a kitchen renovation to finally rid yourself of the 70s Formica and drop ceiling. What part of the job would sound most appealing? The design? The budgeting? The materials research and requisition? The demolition? The installation?

- Another way to access this is to think of the show/movie, *Mission Impossible*. A small team of people worked together to make the impossible possible. Each team member respected and totally counted on the unique talents of the other players, though very different than their own. The key was that each player knew themselves, had worked to master their strengths, and loved the opportunity to put their talents to use (never trying to be a jack-of-all-trades). What would your role be on *Mission Impossible*?

You should end up with a solid list that seems repetitive. That's a good thing! Highlight the words that appear two times or more and watch the words that describe you begin to emerge. I'm so thankful that God gave you all those gifts because I guarantee I'm not good at half of them. We need you in this world to be and do those things!

If you are like most entrepreneurs we work with, your job description does not necessarily match up with your strengths. You probably do all kinds of things because, frankly, there's no one else to do them. This is the life of a small business owner. A common mistake is to spend a lot of time and energy trying to improve upon your weak areas. You'll end up with an improved weakness, not a true strength. There may be people (even your spouse!) that have the strengths that match up perfectly to do those tasks. Let's spend some time to figure out if we can make everybody's life easier.

Remember the Venn diagram you created in Chapter 5 to clarify job responsibilities? I'd like you and your spouse to get together with your strength lists and your Venn diagrams. It's time to compare them. Take your tasks one by one and evaluate the strengths they require. For example, writing blog posts requires creativity as well as wordsmith skills. It may be a good fit for you if you enjoy contemplative tasks, reading, and writing. If you are detail-oriented and enjoy precise hobbies like wood working, blogging may be out of your natural comfort zone. Link the tasks that match up to your strengths (they are usually the ones you like to do the most) and highlight those that are not in your wheelhouse.

Matching Strengths and Responsibilities

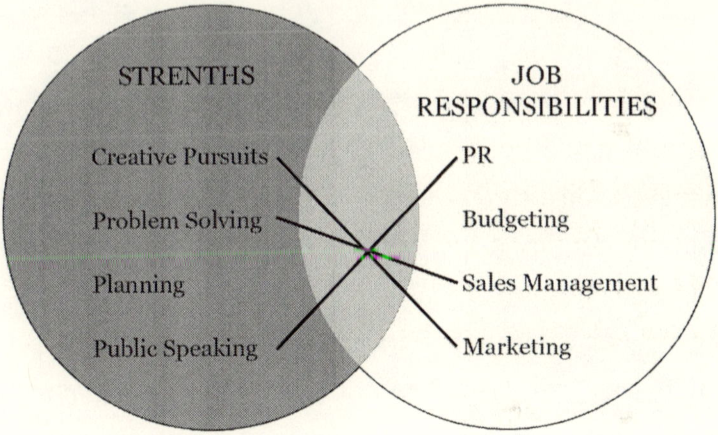

Diagram 7.0

You will both have a bucket of tasks that haven't been assigned. Are there any from his list that jump out at you? Do they seem challenging in a fun way? Maybe some of yours jump out at him. Approach this like you are playing a matching game. Match up the tasks with the strengths without overthinking it. The last thing you need is a lengthy discussion about why it would be impossible to delegate a particular task. Logistics can be figured out later.

At your dinner table, do you ever have leftovers? That's my kids' least favorite meal and I'm sure this list of jobs is feeling just as appetizing. You are probably staring at it thinking, *who in the world is going to do that stuff?* Don't worry. We'll get to that in a minute. For now, enjoy the idea that you may be able to stick to your God-given talents and give your spouse and your employees the same opportunity to shine. Imagine what all of you will be able to do!

THE ART OF DELEGATION

What keeps you from delegating those tasks you are not great at and don't really enjoy? One answer we hear from clients is that they cannot afford to hire help. If you have that thought, spend some time analyzing that choice. You may not be placing nearly enough value on your time. For example, if you are great at bringing in new business, it would make the most sense for you to spend your time doing that activity because it brings so much value to your company. Administrative tasks could be handled by an assistant at minimum wage and free up your time to do the things that give you the most return. There's also a myriad of freelancers that you can hire on a project basis to reduce your workload and help you focus on your strengths. Open your mind to possibilities!

Another fear is that to give away a job means it will probably never get done properly again. Here is a key distinction: Delegate vs. Abdicate. When you delegate a task, you must build in a way to follow up or have the person report to you so that you can be assured the job is done. You are still responsible for the ultimate result; you don't just abdicate that responsibility because you have delegated the job.

The other common reason our clients fail to delegate is that they have such a great work ethic, and would never, ever want to feel they were shirking work. Do you remember Rosie the Riveter? She represented a group of six million women that took over factory jobs when the young men were fighting in World War II. The women didn't hesitate. They just rolled up their sleeves and got to work. I'll bet that you are a lot like that. If you see a task that needs to be done, you get right in there and make sure it's done well. I admire that about you. That grit is what got you where you are in life and in business. But at what cost?

"I feel like I'm losing myself more every day," my friend shared with me over the phone. She works with her husband in Chicago and her life is nonstop. We don't talk often, but when we do we feel safe to reveal all the things that trouble us. "My soul is tired," she said with a long sigh.

"Tell me more," I said, hurting for her.

She paused, working on her wording. "Sometimes I wonder if this is all I am. I wake up early to work, and then I have to rush around and get the kids ready for school. I spend the entire day fixing problems I didn't cause. I'm so sick of everybody else's problems, you know?" she asked, her tone and question seeking validation.

"Of course you are. I would be too," I said, wishing I could reach for her hand.

"Anyway, before I get anything really accomplished I have to stop, go pick up the kids and switch back to mom mode. Then they go to bed and I'm back on my laptop or working through the day with my husband. It just never ends and I'm tired. I'm really tired."

My friend is one of the strongest women I know but success had momentarily defeated her. The cost was too high because it had taken everything that mattered to her. It had taken away her passion for the strategy of business, her joy of parenting, her opportunities to play and live and connect with friends. Of course her soul was tired. Is yours?

We work with clients daily that have fallen into the owner's trap. Early on in their business, they are the only person to do most things. They become true experts on the products and go above and beyond to keep customers happy. This is a beautiful thing until they begin to grow.

Employees usually will not ever have the level of expertise of the owner, and the customers are quick to sniff this out. Problems arise and employees and customers continually seek out the owner to fix the messes. The owner has tried to delegate but it's all blowing up in their face and they think, *I might as well do it myself!* But the owner is only one person. There will be a point when growth plateaus because the owner simply can't do any more. Their soul gets tired.

That's when they call us to sell. They want out. They are done. And we have to break the terrible news that their business's value is much lower than it could be because of their high level of involvement. If the owner is by far the most valuable asset in a company, how can they expect to step out and have the business remain strong, profitable and of interest to a buyer? The diagram below is courtesy of the Value Builder system and it represents the multiple of earnings a client will earn based on their engagement with customers.

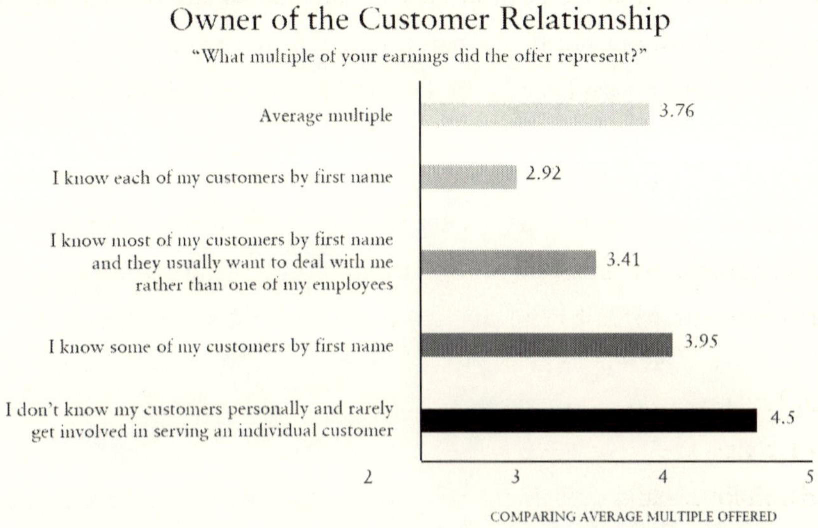

This graph shows the true cost of an owner being too involved, i.e., neglecting their role of training others under them, and implementing systems. If the client is netting $500,000 a year and knows each of their customers by first name, they will be able to sell their business for $1,460,000. If they answer, "I don't know my customers personally and rarely get involved in serving an individual customer," that number will jump to $2,270,000. Stepping away from the day-to-day operations would earn this person over $800,000 more and it will give them their freedom. Win/Win.

Let's figure out how we can make this happen for you. First, you have to change your mindset. In your business model, rather than trying to sell lots of things to lots of people, you are going to need to narrow your focus to one thing that you sell to lots of people. I know that seems counterintuitive. Why narrow your product and service options when you are trying to grow? It's about scalability. You want to become a business that can expand comfortably without taxing you personally.

This is only possible if the product you offer is teachable, valuable and repeatable (you can sell the same thing to the same customer over and over). If you do not design your business to be scalable, you are very, very limited.

We had a client that had a passion for dogs. Her business was around serving them. She did grooming, dog training, and pet sitting. She personally did 90% of the day-to-day work and so we asked her to complete this exercise. She rated each item on a scale of one to ten, then compared the totals. Here are her results.

Service	Teachable	Valuable	Repeatable	Total
Grooming	7	3	9	19
Pet Sitting	9	2	3	14
Training	3	9	1	13

Although training was her most lucrative service, it wasn't as teachable. She offered a specialized system of training that she had learned and perfected over 25 years. It also wasn't a service people used over and over again. Usually they brought their puppies in to learn basic obedience and she never saw them again.

Pet sitting was very teachable but took an inordinate amount of time for the dollar value. They averaged $10-an-hour net profit. Less than minimum wage. She did see repeat customers, but most of them only traveled one or two times a year.

Grooming, however, was very easy to teach and it is repeatable. People brought their dogs in at regular intervals for baths, nail trims and cuts. The dollar value wasn't very high and this concerned her. She did not want to simply raise her price for grooming and compete paw-to-paw with other groomers. She wanted a way to offer more *value*...something that could command a premium price in her market.

We put our heads together and decided to offer a subscription plan. Now she sells a monthly pet spa pass and people can pick a day each month to drop their dog off for a full grooming and pampering experience. She has a team of people that can give customers top notch service and they have grown to four locations. She hired a manager for each location and spends most of her free time enjoying her own dogs.

Make it Happen (20 Minutes)

Sound good? Let's do it. Make a list of all of your products and services and rate them. If you are more visual, you can plot your scores on a bar graph or an X Y axis. The scores will speak for themselves. It will be painful to let go of things you have built from the ground up. You will fight the urge to keep everything. Just keep remembering your goals of freedom and growth. This will get you there.

If this seems difficult because you offer products rather than services, think of how you might be able to wrap a service around your product. For example, there is a running shoe company that sells Nike, Reebok, etc. The owner offers weekly running clinics for his customers. He brings in experts to speak on subjects that matter to them and then the group heads out for a run together. He doesn't charge for the clinic but it makes them "stickier." They are loyal to his brand and it has helped him to increase sales enough to expand to ten locations.

It's time to take back your life. You've got this!

WHO IS IN CONTROL?

I've always found that the easiest part of business is in the planning. The hardest part is letting go and letting God. I once heard someone say, "We plan, God laughs." It makes me think of the time my kids planned to make some extra money by putting on a "daredevil show" for people walking by the house. They had set up boxes in big stacks and were crashing through them on their bikes. Tickets would be $5 apiece and it came with a free can of Coke. I couldn't imagine anyone paying $5 to watch them crash into boxes but I let them try. They came into the house an hour later, completely dejected that no one wanted to stop to watch (let alone pay for!) their show.

I could have intervened in their plan. I could have told them all the reasons it wouldn't work. I chose instead to let them experience it so that they could learn from it. I believe that God does the same with us. He doesn't laugh because He wants to harm us—He laughs because He has even better plans than we could ever imagine.

And yet, when I try to apply this same wisdom to my life it seems so much harder.

My husband and I were struggling financially and I wanted to believe it was in my power to fix it. I reconciled the bank account three times and three different ways. I lowered our credit card payments, cut back on everything but the necessities, and still the number stared its ugly stare right back at me. We only had one month of money left and the deals that were in the pipeline were tenuous at best. Suddenly, the numbers on the screen blurred because of the tears that welled up in my eyes. I couldn't understand why God wasn't answering very specific prayers. I was doing everything right, wasn't I? I felt an immense need to take control and my anxiety began to spiral. I got up out of the office chair and sought out a hug from my husband.

"Let's pray," he said simply as he held me close. "God, my beautiful wife is hurting right now and we are both at a loss about what to do. Give her strength, God. Bless her with your wisdom and perspective. Help her find time in her day to spend time with you. Maybe go to the jetty and just watch the boats and spend some time with you. We thank you for your love and grace. In Jesus' name, Amen." He pulled out of the hug and suggested I take an hour to myself. And that's exactly what I did.

With a beautiful view of the water, I took out my journal and a favorite pen and sat down to write and think and pray and listen. But five minutes later, a very vocal older man plopped down his chair right next to me. He complained about the weather, the fishermen, the boaters and anything else he could think of, and tried over and over again to engage me in conversation. I tried to politely smile and go back to my journal but it wasn't working. He kept talking no matter what I did or said. My frustration was mounting until he yelled, "What in the hell are they thinking!?" My eyes shot up to see a yacht with the engine stalled.

The jetty is where a narrow waterway leads from the Intracoastal Waterway into the Gulf of Mexico. It's lined with rocks on both sides and the yacht was inching its way toward the rocks. I felt a gentle urging from God to pay attention. The young men on the boat were obviously inexperienced boaters and they lowered the anchor but not enough. The boat continued to drift. Men on both sides yelled out to the boaters, "You have to let out more line! The anchor didn't catch!!" The young men rushed back to the front of the boat to try to set the anchor. They uncoiled more line and let it loose. As soon as the anchor caught, the engine restarted.

I felt God impressing on my heart, "I am your anchor but I cannot protect you from the rocks if you don't give me enough line." I almost lost my breath—that's how struck I was with God's wisdom. The one thing I did have control of was my trust in Him. I had to give Him the line. I felt a tear drip down my face and suddenly was aware that I was crying tears of relief. He had never stopped holding me in His hands.

When I got home, I checked to see if there were verses about anchors and found this from Hebrews 6:19: "We have this hope as an anchor for our soul." My pastor told me that an anchor needs three times the depth of the water to be secured. Three times. That's a lot of line. That's a lot of trust. And yet, I knew at that moment that it was safe to let go.

He's the anchor for your soul, too. He is in control of every aspect of your life. You can trust Him even when the situation seems impossible. It's not always easy; the things that God asks us to experience are daunting. I love the line in the movie, *Evan Almighty*, when Evan, a modern-day Noah who has been asked to build an ark, says, "I know, I know. You only do things because you love me. But could you try loving me a little less?"

We all want life to be easy but, to put it simply, it's not. God has much bigger things in mind than we could ever begin to imagine but He can't make them happen when we wrestle control from Him. Here are a few things to do when you feel yourself pulling up anchor.

Make it Happen (20 Minutes)

- **Make a Daily Date with God**

  Letting go of control is not a one-time thing. It is a constant battle, especially during times of high stress. But we have to remember that we are incapable of making decisions as well as God does. The prophet Isaiah writes, "For my thoughts are not your thoughts, neither are your ways my ways, declares the Lord. For as the heavens are higher than the earth, so are my ways higher than your ways and my thoughts than your thoughts."

This statement is not to make you feel small, it is meant to liberate you. Schedule time every day to spend with your Savior. Start the day by breathing in the promise in Matthew 11:30 to make your burden light. Business pressures, family issues, financial stress, addiction...there isn't anything He hasn't seen or doesn't know. Feel yourself physically handing your pain to Him and envision Him taking it from you and turning it to dust. *Thank you, Lord, for giving me a sense of peace.* Praying as if it's already happened secures your trust in Him.

Once a day may not be enough if you are in deep, rough waters. Each time you feel yourself drifting toward the rocky shores of life, give Him more line. Repeat the exercise as many times as it takes to regain your equilibrium.

- **Seek Out Each Other**

When you are in a high-stress moment, you can't see the forest for the trees. Your husband or another woman of faith will be able to provide a listening ear and a new perspective. Lean on them and go to God together. The Lord promises that "When two or more gather in my name, there am I with them" (Matthew 18:20).

I know you want to appear strong. I know you don't want to burden anyone else with your "stuff." I challenge you to get vulnerable and ask for those prayers. The Lord will hear them and act on them, I assure you.

WHO ARE YOU WITHOUT YOUR BUSINESS?

Have you seen the *LEGO Batman* movie? There's a scene where Batman hurts the Joker's feelings by saying that the Joker means nothing to him. The Joker decides to get himself put in jail so that Batman can realize how much of his life revolves around stopping the Joker's shenanigans. Once Joker is in jail, Batman becomes depressed. He finds himself alone in his giant lair with every gadget and comfort he could ever desire but still feels unfulfilled. He walks the streets aimlessly and even spies on the Joker in jail because he misses the challenge of defeating him. His life has no purpose without the Joker because that alone defined him.

Business owners and Batman can have a lot in common. We get completely absorbed in the growth of our business. We have our own Joker in our competitors (or other dragons to slay) and thrive on winning and succeeding. Our identity easily gets tied into our companies and our culture supports that mentality.

The first thing we are asked when we meet someone new is, "What do you do?" It's meant as a polite conversation starter, a way to find commonalities. But subconsciously we are measuring someone's worth.

When I stopped working to stay home with my little ones I remember feeling immense discomfort when someone asked that question. My husband would sometimes answer for me and say, "She has the hardest job in the world. She takes care of our family." While I felt proud of that calling, I let the reaction of others define how I felt about myself. They would quickly dismiss me as "just a mom" and move on to discussing my husband's career at great length.

I began to conform to their expectations and say things like, "I used to be a marketing director of a software company but chose to stay at home with my kids." Their eyes would light up as if to say, *I guess she is worth something*, and they would then engage me in conversation.

You may feel the same pressure as an entrepreneur. How in the world can you narrow down all that you do in the length of a tweet? Shannon Compton, Financial Strategist, has a funny way of describing her reaction to this dreaded question: "'It's nice to meet you... what do you do for a living?' That is my least favorite question of them all. Entrepreneurs, can I get an *Amen*? How in the world do I describe myself? I am part Certified Financial Planner professional, part branding and marketing expert, part product creator, part expert at connecting people together, part writer, and part speaker... not to mention I can make a mean risotto."

You've worked hard to start or buy your business. You've poured your life into making it a success, right? But at some point, you may want to begin to step away from the day-to-day operations. At some point, you may want to explore more of what life has to offer and less of what your business has to offer. At that juncture, fear may settle in your heart and the question may arise, *who am I without this business?* The world expects success and defines your worth on what you do. If we forget who we are living our life to please, we can get trapped in that definition.

My parents sold their software company to my sister and brother-in-law in 2012, making it possible for my parents to retire. My dad, however, had a really hard time letting it go. He asked that he keep his company email address "just in case" and stopped by the office frequently to check in. He would walk around and talk to employees, check on projects and go out to lunch with the friends he had made while he worked there. Later he admitted that he didn't know who he was without being a business owner. He felt lost. He felt as if he wasn't bringing value into the world by being retired. His whole identity was his work.

That's heartbreaking. I don't want that to happen to you. You are not your business. You were created by our God to do amazing things and your business is only one component of your life. Let's spend some time exploring who you *are* instead of focusing on what you *do*.

Make it Happen (30 Minutes)

1. **You Have a Beautiful Life Beyond Your Business.**

   Relationships are the key to life. Spend time cultivating them. I've had too many entrepreneurs say to me, "I just wish I had more of a life!"

   Life is there for the taking if you want it. Schedule lunches with friends, have a big Sunday dinner and invite families that mean a lot to you. Create these kinds of opportunities for fellowship. A few hours a week can do wonders. Feeling too drained for social engagements? Send out one card a week telling a loved one you are thinking of them. Drop a note in your kids' backpacks. Send a few texts to friends in the morning asking how that interview went or if they got that deal they've been praying for. There are many ways to simply connect with someone else. Get creative and intentional. You will never regret taking the time to grow your relationships.

2. **You Have Spiritual Gifts**

Did you know that you are gifted? No matter what the IQ test says, you have been gifted since birth with specific talents that are meant to be used for God's kingdom.

"We have different gifts, according to the grace given to each of us. If your gift is prophesying, then prophesy in accordance with your faith; if it is serving, then serve; if it is teaching, then teach; if it is to encourage, then give encouragement; if it is giving, then give generously; if it is to lead, do it diligently; if it is to show mercy, do it cheerfully" (Romans 12:6-8).

That list is only a sample of the myriad of gifts listed in the Bible. I challenge you to take a spiritual gift test online and uncover your strengths. Gifttest.com offers a ten minute survey that reveals your giftedness.

Once you fully understand your gifts, pray to God to show you how He'd like you to use them. Here's a prayer from my heart to yours:

Dear merciful Savior, Thank you for giving me the gift of ________. I know you have amazing plans for me, God! Help me to see what you have planned for me. Bring me opportunities to serve you that fall within my giftedness. Make it obvious, God, so that I don't question it for a second but instead embrace it fully. Help me to change the world for you and with you. In Jesus' mighty name, amen.

3. **You are a Child of God**

   You are, first and foremost, a child of God. That is more powerful than any business empire you can grow. Knowing how God sees you is a powerful way to shape how you see yourself. Here are a few verses that embody your identity in Christ.

- You have been blessed with every spiritual blessing in the heavenly places.

Blessed is the God and Father of our Lord Jesus Christ, who has blessed us with every spiritual blessing in the heavenly realms in Christ (Ephesians 1:3).

- You are chosen, holy, and blameless before God

For he chose us in Christ before the foundation of the world that we may be holy and unblemished in his sight in love (Ephesians 1:4).

- You are a temple of the Holy Spirit

Do you not know that your bodies are temples of the Holy Spirit, who is in you, whom you have received from God? You are not your own (1 Corinthians 6:19).

This prayer from Bekah Jane Pogue author of *Choosing Real* is my prayer for you:

God, may I be rooted in Your truth, knowing my ultimate value and worth are found in You. As I live out this truth, may my identity overflow into all I do and say, reflecting my Maker. May I know confidence and security when jobs, zip codes, and communities change. When my spouse doesn't understand me, or my purpose seems foggy, or my kids are going nuts, help me remember who I am in You. Amen.

9

Reflect, Reset, Give Back

For I know the plans I have for you,
declares the Lord.
Plans to prosper you and not to harm you,
plans to give you hope and a future.

Jeremiah 29:11

TRANSFORMATION

Did you know that if you help a butterfly out of its chrysalis, that butterfly may not survive? They need the struggle of pushing out of the safety of the cocoon to strengthen their wings enough for flight. You are that butterfly. You have begun to see the possibilities of a new life. You have dreamed big dreams and prayed for God to make them happen for you. The next step is embracing transformation. Scripture repeatedly encourages us toward transformation.

"Therefore, if anyone is in Christ, the new creation has come: The old has gone, the new is here!" (2 Corinthians 5:17).

"Do not conform to the pattern of this world, but be transformed by the renewing of your mind. Then you will be able to test and approve what God's will is—his good, pleasing and perfect will" (Romans 12:2).

"I will give you a new heart and put a new spirit in you; I will remove from you your heart of stone and give you a heart of flesh" (Ezekiel 36:26).

It sounds so easy when we read these verses, but transformation is anything but easy. We have spent our life doing things a certain way and to face significant change invokes fear. We are comfortable in this life even if it isn't authentic. We know what to expect from day to day and we tell ourselves that that is enough. Changing our hearts, beliefs, and lives feels insurmountable.

I have a friend that does interior design as a hobby. When people walk into her house or her office for the first time, they actually gasp. When she sold her last house, the realtor asked her to move all the furniture out because "the amazing décor is too intimidating for the women buyers." Her hobby's result is that good. People will say, "This looks like a page in a magazine!" or "Who decorated this space for you?" Her face reddens as she admits that she did this in her spare time. The rest of her life is spent running a multi-million dollar software company.

Are you a decorator trapped in a software company? We live so much of our lives saying yes and following a path because that's the way the cards fell. It seems like the easiest thing to do, it's what we went to college to do, it's the thing that you've always done. You may be a shining star in your field (as my friend is in software) but it doesn't necessarily light your fire anymore. You don't have to keep trudging through this jungle.

If you are honest with yourself, is it possible you have been believing you are "not enough" or that you are not truly the magnificent child of God who can transform into a beautiful butterfly that can fly to any desired destination?

What if you knew that Jesus would give you the strength, insights and wisdom to be living a joyous and fulfilled life? What if the first step to living authentically was simply asking for His help, each and every day? "Jesus did not leave His followers wondering *if* we could succeed or have the help we need to make the changes! He knows exactly what everyone needs, and He is ready to give it to you. One reason people fail to overcome and make lasting changes in their lives is that they try to overcome their human weaknesses on their own—not recognizing their dire need for constant help from God through the Holy Spirit," shares the United Church of God on www.ucg.org.

In my own church, I have seen a beautiful and powerful example of transformation. Billy Day gave me permission to share this story with you. Billy came to our church a few months after overcoming addiction. He started as our sound guy, quietly working in the sound booth during band practice and Sunday services. But God had bigger plans for this man of God. First, we lost a guitar player and he stepped up to play in our worship band. No longer only "behind the scenes," Billy started to be more known and appreciated by the congregation. Then, suddenly, our worship leader resigned. No one in the church was prepared for that change, and we all had to remind ourselves that God would see us through.

My husband was the head elder at the time and felt led to ask Billy to fill that role. He accepted, and the church has been blessed by his talent, encouragement, and faith. He has transformed into a faithful and loving leader and has risen in our church as a true inspiration and testimony of the power of the Holy Spirit.

Billy explains his transformation this way: "I think one of the things that's most remarkable about my transformation is how God had to break me down to my core. Prior to the change, I had become totally ineffective. I couldn't achieve even the simplest goals. Once I became "emptied" or "stripped away," I finally began to feel true forgiveness in my heart for myself and those who'd hurt me. The change was profound. Suddenly goals were attainable and I was achieving things that I never could have dreamed of. Sometimes God has to break us down so that He can re-purpose our lives for a new direction."

"Change is about using external influences to modify actions to achieve desired results. Transformation is about modifying beliefs so that natural actions achieve the desired results," writes author, John Palinkas.

Make it Happen (20 Minutes)

Is the spirit beckoning you to "empty yourself" so that you can be more, do more, transform?

We've freed up your time, now let's emerge from your cocoon of "the way you've always done it" and begin your transformation. I have three questions for you to answer. These are going to take some soul-searching and I need you to be really honest with yourself. Get a beautiful journal out for this exercise. Your dreams deserve a sacred place.

1. **What Do You Want?**

   Close your eyes and see your life for what it can be. Write it down with vivid descriptions. Draw a picture if you sketch. Know that you cannot say a "wrong" thing. Your journal will not judge you.

   Beware of self-limiting thoughts. You will want to talk yourself out of these things because they seem silly or unattainable. Write down those fears and doubts as you go on sticky notes but don't let them mar the pages of your journal. We will address them later.

Here are a few questions to spark your thinking:

- How can your character grow? Do you need God to help you cultivate more patience, optimism, joy?
- What dreams do you want to make happen through His strength?
- Do you want more time with your children? Maybe there is a book in your heart just waiting to be written? Do you want to open a new business with a totally different focus?
- Are there any new beauty or fashion trends that sound fun? What about that new way to do your makeup or hair you've been dying to try?
- What do your days look like? Do you want to spend every morning doing yoga on the beach and every afternoon having coffee with a friend?

List anything and everything. No dream is too big or too small. Get it on paper. Remember this quote from Walt Disney, "It's kind of fun to do the impossible." Writing it down is the first step to making the impossible happen.

2. **Who Can I help?**

God's hands do all things big and small. Think about the causes that tug at your heart. Think about the people you see all the time that could use some love. I bake for our church once a month. It's not a big thing but I know it gives people a little bit of joy to sit around a table after church eating my coffee cake. It can be that simple.

Say a small prayer before you write anything down. God will lead you. *Dear Lord, I thank you for opening my life up to new possibilities. I thank you for the gifts you have given me. Reveal to me how I can help those I love and those I have never even met. Fill my heart with their needs so that I can fill them, Lord. In Jesus' mighty name, Amen.*

Write down a quick list of skills and then apply it to a cause. Do you knit? Maybe the pediatric unit of the hospital could use some handmade blankets. Are you a natural with kids? Maybe you can help out at an after school program. Keep in communication with God on this one. He may reveal a need you never even anticipated.

Finding Opportunities to Serve

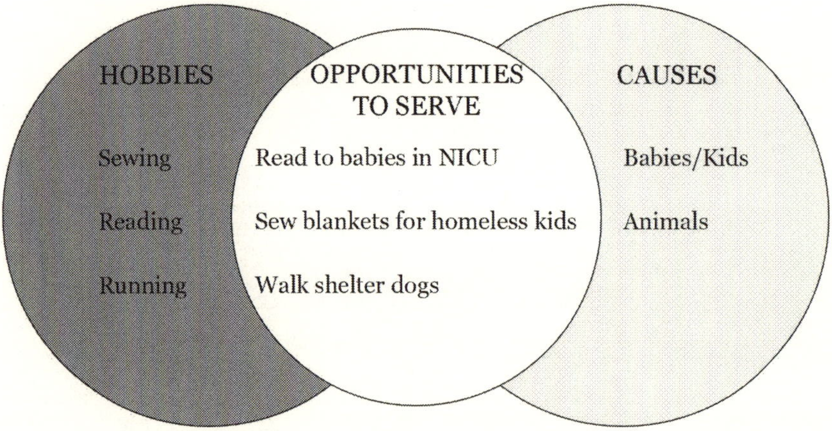

Diagram 8.0

3. **Why Not Now?**

I don't mean this question in the clichéd way it can be used. There may be very valid reasons why you can't backpack through Europe or launch a new business at this very moment. The key is that you must differentiate between obstacles and self-limiting beliefs. Obstacles are things that make the path more difficult to traverse. We may be unable to have five acres of land because we haven't sold our current home. That's an obstacle that can be overcome. A self-limiting belief, in contrast, is filled with emotion. I may believe I can't have a house with five acres because we won't ever be able to sell our house. I have given up on the possibility and, therefore, my dream. I *can* sell the house but believing it's impossible will keep me from even trying.

I'm sure you wrote out a few fears and doubts on sticky notes during step one. Revisit those and list out any others that jump in your mind. Now let them sit overnight. No cheating!

Take them out the next morning and prayerfully consider each one again. Are they truths from God or limitations from your mind? Are you really unable to do yoga on the beach because you are "too out of shape" or is that the best reason in the world to start? The enemy will give you a million reasons to stop this process. He will tell you that you can't. He will insist that you are being selfish or that you are wasting your time. God's voice will be encouraging and loving. He sits back and looks at you with joy and wonder. Crumble up and toss those sticky notes from the enemy. They are lies. Keep only those that are true obstacles to overcome and write them down in your journal. We will tackle those next in our storyboarding session.

GIVING BACK

"For we are his workmanship, having been created in Christ Jesus for good works that God prepared beforehand so we may do them" (Ephesians 2:10).

Our lives are so much bigger than our businesses. We can forget that if we become fixated on our day to day. Get the kids ready, get them to school, start the line-up of conference calls, meetings and lunch and coffee dates, get home and start dinner, clean-up, then get the kids to bed. Watch TV, check email, go to bed and start it all over again. It's exhausting. When do we even have time to give back when our lives are so full? If we are not careful, our world shrinks and we forget that anything else exists beyond our own experiences.

Giving back helps others but it also reduces anxiety and depression, increases your overall health and joy, connects you to your calling, and even increases your job performance. "Charitable work literally makes the heart grow stronger. Individuals with coronary artery disease who participate in volunteer activities after suffering a heart attack report a reduction in despair and depression, and that, in turn, drives down mortality and adds years to life. It's also true that those who volunteer have fewer incidents of heart disease in the first place," reports the Corporation for National & Community Service.

It is almost as if God designed our bodies to want to serve others. Interestingly, the research shows that we only need to spend two hours a week devoted to giving back to reap these health benefits. We all have two hours, even in the busiest seasons of our lives.

Wondering what you can do to give back? I firmly believe that your cause can only be revealed through prayer and life experience. "Praise be to the God and Father of our Lord Jesus Christ, the Father of compassion and the God of all comfort, who comforts us in all our troubles, so that we can comfort those in any trouble with the comfort we ourselves receive from God" (2 Corinthians 1:3-4). We all go through some really tough things in this world and find ourselves asking God why. Why would he put us through all this pain? Why did that bad thing have to happen? I don't have all the answers for that one, but I do know that we have an opportunity to turn a negative experience into a beautiful and empathetic ministry. Who better to serve than someone who has walked that journey and come out the other side whole? Maybe you didn't handle it well, maybe you did. It doesn't matter. The only thing that matters is that you feel emotionally connected to that cause. God placed that in your heart. Trust it.

Our third child was a preemie and spent two weeks in the neonatal intensive care unit (NICU). It was incredibly stressful but we had constant support from family and friends. They brought me food, toiletries, tiny little preemie clothes for our baby girl, and even gave me their Netflix and Audible passwords so I could have a bit of distraction. I walked by the other NICU rooms day after day on my way to the coffee station and saw new mamas sitting there all by themselves. It broke my heart. I wanted to be there for those families more than anything. I felt strongly that God was calling me to help them.

I prayed about it all the time but felt that God was telling me to wait. I focused on raising three kids under five but I constantly felt this undercurrent of urgency. I felt that every day that passed was another mom in the NICU feeling scared and alone. I liken it to the feeling you have when your newborn cries; you just have to get to them and soothe them.

One year after my daughter's birth, God said "go!" to my spirit. I began the process of starting my own non-profit but I was chasing my tail. I jumped from one thing to the next (Website! No, 501C3 status! No, product lines!). I sat in the post office parking lot, ready to register for a P.O. Box and called Dane for advice. "I'm spinning in circles," I told him. "I am so overwhelmed!"

"You do great with checklists. There's got to be something online if you Google, 'steps to starting a non-profit,'" he suggested.

Great advice. Let's get a second on that one. I called my mom and started my tale of woe from the top. "I just don't feel like I'm getting anywhere!" I bemoaned. She, remarkably, said the same thing Dane had said. Find a checklist. And so I did.

I know now that God was speaking through them because the first item on the list was to find out if there was a non-profit in my geographic region with the same idea. Unlike businesses, non-profits do not do well when there are duplicate services. They need to be the go-to for a specific area. I was sure that nothing existed but I do like a good checklist. I went to Guidestar.org to search and, lo and behold, the only organization in the country was in Tampa, just 50 miles away.

I reached out to the organization and they asked me to fill out a lengthy application that included hospital statistics. I fought through the hospital bureaucracy with a tenacity I had never known was within me. I sent the application back within a few days and said a quiet prayer for His will to be done.

I later learned that they had never had anyone complete the application despite having sent it out many times. The founder, Heather Barrow, called me and said it was interesting that I had reached out when I did.

Their Board had just voted to allow their first expansion to a hospital in California and they were thinking about how to continue expanding their services. She said my timing was perfect, although I knew that it was His timing that was perfect.

I met with the organization, High Risk Hope, and I fought back tears when I walked into their office. "This is like looking at a dream come true," I shared with them. They had done every single thing that I had envisioned. Their shelves were lined with toiletries and small items to bring the families comfort during their NICU stay. Beautiful bags with sparkly bows overflowed with handmade baby blankets, hats, and information to help answer the families' questions. It was incredible.

High Risk Hope didn't have the funding to expand to Sarasota Memorial Hospital but they encouraged me to get out there and raise the money to make it happen. I wasn't dissuaded because I could focus on one thing, fundraising. I didn't have to worry about websites and P.O. Boxes anymore. I could get to the heart of providing these care packages to the families.

Heather was a constant source of encouragement as she shared all the things she had done to launch High Risk Hope. She suggested sending a handwritten note out to everyone on my Christmas card list telling them what I hoped to do for the families. I spent hours writing 80 notes but I never felt discouraged. It was quite the opposite. I felt more determined and hopeful that the money would come in with each note I wrote. That Christmas, I celebrated the first $1,000 toward helping those families.

I put together several fundraisers but the craziest was the one that started with a popsicle. My oldest son was outside on a sizzling hot Florida day and our neighbor come out to walk her dog. She was talking about the heat and my son offered a popsicle. She said she would love one after her walk and he ran inside to grab one out of the freezer. I went with him to deliver the treat and we all sat on her porch enjoying the respite. She asked what I had been up to and I shared the vision for High Risk Hope in Sarasota. She stared at me for a long time and said, "You know, I have a family foundation. I'd love to give you your start." A month later, a check came in the mail for $3,000. I was in awe of God's constant support of this mission.

It took a year, but God opened every door to help me raise the $20,000 it took to provide a year of service to Sarasota Memorial's NICU. I walked through those hospital doors two years after I had left them and my hands were full of hope for those mamas. I was overwhelmed. Overcome. Humbled that He had trusted me to be His hands and a representative of His heart to these families.

I want you to be overwhelmed, overcome, and humbled. You were put on this earth for a purpose that only God can reveal. You may have already found it (what a blessing!) but if you haven't, let's ask the Lord to bring it to you.

Dear Lord, my friend is seeking your heart. I thank you for preparing an amazing purpose for her. I thank you for giving her very specific skills that will serve your kingdom. I thank you for reassuring her that the struggles in her life have not been in vain. Show her, with great clarity, how she can be your hands and your heart in this world. Show her how she can shine your light into the deepest darkest corners of this earth. I can't wait to see how you change the world through her. In Jesus' mighty name, Amen.

First delivery of care packages to neonatal intensive care (NICU), December 2015

STORYBOARDING SUCCESS

This is not your dress rehearsal. This life is yours for the taking. You have dreams and they are just beginning to see the light of day. Some are big, some are small. Some feel frivolous and some feel world-changing. You've had time to make some happen but many of them have been shoved aside as you deal with the practicalities of life. No more. Today is the day to breathe life back into your dreams and begin the process of making them a reality.

Do your dreams appear as high-resolution HD images, or have they been ignored for so long they are badly faded and a challenge to bring front and center? You need to make them real. The Reticular Activating System (RAS) lies at the base of your brain and filters all the millions of bits of data our brain receives each day. Sounds, tastes, colors, and images bombard us and the RAS only lets in the things it deems important. How does it decide what's important? Your focus.

Here's a tiny example of your RAS at work. I want you to think of a color. Any color will do. Now put the book down and scan the room. Does that color jump out at you? Your RAS is filtering out all the other colors and helping you to notice the color you chose. Can you imagine the power of that focus once you decide to go after a dream?

"That is why goal-setting is so important. It creates a category in your reticular activating system, and you start noticing anything and everything that will help you accomplish the goal," explains Mark Batterson in *The Circle Maker*. "Prayer is important for the same reason. It sanctifies your RAS so you notice what God wants you to notice. The more you pray, the more you notice."

As I began this book, it seemed that articles, songs, and examples of marriage based on God, priority-setting, and business success flooded my Facebook feed, my inbox, and my daily conversations. I didn't subscribe to anything new or even tell many people about this project, and yet God used a spiritual highlighter to show me everything I needed to complete it. The very first day I sat down to write, God gave me this verse through my devotional, Daily Guideposts. "May you be strengthened with all power, according to His glorious might, for all endurance and patience with joy, giving thanks to the Father, who has qualified you to share in the inheritance of the saints in light" (Colossians 1:11-12).

I heard that as a promise. My prayer every single day was a prayer of thanks for that promise. I thanked Him for strengthening me with all His power, for giving me endurance, patience and joy and, mostly, for qualifying me to share in His glorious light. And you know what? He's done all of those things each and every day.

He wants to make your dreams and goals happen, too. Remember how we used storyboarding to make decisions? We are going to use it again to brainstorm and free up your thinking. This is a Possibilities Session. God can make the impossible happen. Do you want to get your scuba certification? Run with the bulls in Spain? Raise $10,000 for the Humane Society? Take your kids to the Super Bowl? No dream is too big for God.

You can do this on your own but I encourage you to do this with your spouse. I love doing it together because "when two or more gather in my name, there I am with them" (Matthew 18:20). Your husband's goals will probably be very different from yours but that gives you insight into his heart. Dane and I have some separate goals and some that overlap—we would both love to go on a mission trip and because we know that, we can both seek opportunities to fulfill that dream and check it off our life list. You will find the same thing happening and will be able to cheer each other on toward achieving great things.

Before you begin the session, I encourage you to pray for God to show you what He would like to see you do. This life is for His glory, not ours. Each item on your list should reflect His heart and His purposes for you. I love this line from the praise song, "Lead me to the Cross." It says, "Lord, I lay me down. Rid me of myself. I belong to you." This life belongs to Him. Here's a prayer to center your heart before you begin.

My sweet Lord, you can do the impossible. You can turn water into wine and raise people from the dead. I am amazed by you. I thank you for giving me a purpose in this world and I know you will use me to do the impossible. Show me what you want me to do, God. Shine a light on the things that will fill my soul and build my relationships. Let me always give you the glory for making these goals happen, Lord. Let me shout your praises into this world with everything I say and do. In Jesus' mighty name, Amen.

Ready? Okay, let's go. I like to use a mini storyboarding kit for these types of sessions. Grab a file folder, some colorful scented markers, and 2x2 sticky notes. If you or your spouse is a kinesthetic thinker, grab some Play-Doh or Thinking Putty. Your brain will be more focused when your hands are busy.

Grab those sticky notes and list out these header cards:

Family Goals

Business Goals

Experience Goals

Travel Goals

Financial Goals

Physical Goals

Learning Goals

Character Goals

Ministry Goals

Feel free to add any others that are important to you. I personally have "Homeschooling Goals" on my list because that is part of the legacy I'm hoping to leave. Imagine you are breaking your life into categories and make sure there is a card representing each component on the board.

Review the goals that you have listed out and make sure they meet these four benchmarks:

- Measurable

  You know this one, right? "Work out more" isn't a great goal because it isn't defined. What does "work out" entail and what is "more"? How do you know you've achieved it? The best part of setting a goal is achieving it. You deserve that feeling! "Run in and complete a 5K race by the time I am 45" is an example of a goal with parameters that are measurable.

- Deadline-Driven

  Notice that the goal above has an age (a "by when") attached to it. When your brain sees a deadline, it feels pressure to close the gap between what you want and what you have. It's driven to make it happen for you. Put dates on each goal, even if they are 20 years out.

- Go Big or Go Home

  We often underestimate what we can do in the course of five years, let alone an entire lifetime. I read about famous adventurer John Goddard the other day. He sat under a tree at age 15 and listed out 127 life goals. They were wide-ranging and far flung and yet he accomplished virtually everything on his list including climbing Mt. Vesuvius and "lighting a match with a .22 rifle." This is a time for you to disconnect practicality. Use your imagination as you did when you were a child. Go big and be amazed.

- Consider Others

  Your goals have the power to grow and change your relationships, bring joy to others, and show them that they truly are a priority. We have a goal to take each of our kids on a "coming of age" trip to Europe. This isn't simply to go on a cool trip. It's an opportunity to teach them how to navigate in a foreign country, gain a heart for all the people in God's world, and understand and embrace other cultures. I cannot express how much I look forward to making these memories together with my children. I know it will impact our lives forever.

  You might want a vacation home. That's a fantastic goal…AND, how can you use that home to bless others? Think beyond your own growth and ask God to show you opportunities outside of your own satisfaction.

Are all of your goals measurable, deadline driven, BIG, and taking others into consideration? If not, just make a few adjustments to your wording. If you said, "Spend more time with the kids," you can change that to, "Spend 15 focused minutes a day with each child." We use sticky notes for a reason. Just take off the ones that don't work and replace them!

Take a step back and look at these lists. How will you feel if you accomplish even half of those goals? What about all of them? You can and will with God's help. This life is whatever you make it. Dream big and pray hard.

EMBRACING THE POSSIBILITIES

"We have always held to the hope, the belief, the conviction that there is a better life, a better world, beyond the horizon." —Franklin D. Roosevelt
You have done a lot of work. You have been real with yourself and your husband. You have set boundaries, increased your communication skills, dreamed big and begun to let go and let God. The stage is set for greatness, my friend.

Entrepreneurs are not faint-hearted. You are certainly not lacking in guts or moxie but I must warn you, self-doubt will creep in as you work to redesign your life. I invite you to prepare a preemptive strike against the enemy.

Failure will happen as you explore new ways of living. What if I told you that failure is necessary, even likely? What if I asked you to begin to celebrate those failures instead of hiding from them? That would be a true paradigm shift or, "a fundamental change in approach or underlying assumptions." And yet some of the greatest success stories are rooted in failure.

Thomas Edison famously tried 10,000 filaments before finding one that would light the light bulb. He essentially failed his way to success but we focus only on the accomplishment. The process of inventing the first light bulb was painful and rife with disappointment and yet Edison said, "I have not failed. I've just found 10,000 ways that won't work. Many of life's failures are people who did not realize how close they were to success when they gave up."

Sara Blakely, founder of Spanx and the first American 20-something-year-old woman self-made billionaire, tells a story of her father encouraging her and her brother to share failures at the dinner table. He would ask them what they failed at that day and if they didn't have anything to share, he expressed disappointment.

I saw an interview where she gave the example of sadly confessing that she did not make the cut for the cheerleading squad at school. Her dad reacted not with disappointment but with excitement and pride. He quickly shifted her perspective from her having failed to her having tested the outer edge of her abilities and discovered useful information about herself.

"What he did was redefine failure for my brother and me," Blakely told CNN's Anderson Cooper. "And instead of failure being the outcome, failure became not trying. And it forced me at a young age to want to push myself so much further out of my comfort zone."

Soon after graduating from Florida State University, she spent two years having manufacturers slam the door in her face before she found one that would produce her idea for women's undergarments. Do you think she would have been able to persevere and keep trying if she let those failures define her? (We'd be a lot lumpier in our cocktail dresses if that would've happened!)

It's embarrassing to fail. It hits our confidence and temporarily debilitates us. We internalize it and begin to believe lies like, "You are never going to succeed," or "You don't even know what you're doing." Those self-limiting beliefs are from the enemy. You will need the Lord and each other to lift you up and remind you who you are and all you are capable of doing with God's help.

Following our big dreams can lead not only to personal success but to contributing to God's work in big ways. Since its inception in 2006, the Spanx by Sara Blakely Foundation has donated millions of dollars to charities around the world, focusing on charities that empower underserved women and girls.

"Failure then becomes a tutor, not a judge. In the presence of freedom, we learn from failures instead of being intimidated by them. In the absence of condemnation, confidence in how God can use you mounts," writes Dennis Rainey on FamilyLife.com.

I love the song "Voice of Truth" by Casting Crowns. These words are a balm to my soul when I face a situation that requires a leap of faith.

Oh what I would do to have
The kind of faith it takes
To climb out of this boat I'm in
Onto the crashing waves

To step out of my comfort zone
Into the realm of the unknown where Jesus is
And He's holding out His hand

But the waves are calling out my name
And they laugh at me
Reminding me of all the times
I've tried before and failed
The waves they keep on telling me
Time and time again. "Boy, you'll never win!"
"You'll never win!"

But the voice of truth tells me a different story
The voice of truth says, "Do not be afraid!"
The voice of truth says, "This is for My glory"
Out of all the voices calling out to me
I will choose to listen and believe the voice of truth

Listen to the voice of truth. Embrace the possibilities that God has planned for you. You glorify Him when you pray through a difficult disappointment and place your trust in God's sovereign will.

Make it Happen (30 Minutes)

Did you know that there are over 3,500 promises in the Bible? Your greatest strength will come as you rest on God's promises for you. I encourage you to find a promise and call it yours. Here are a few of His promises that I hold dear:

"For I know the plans I have for you. Plans to prosper you and not to harm you. Plans to give you hope and a future" (Jeremiah 29:11).

"The Lord will fight for you; you need only to be still" (Exodus 14:14).

"...but those who hope in the Lord will renew their strength. They will soar on wings like eagles; they will run and not grow weary, they will walk and not be faint" (Isaiah 40:31).

"I can do all things through Christ who strengthens me" (Philippians 4:13).

There is a promise for every situation, every challenge, every set-back. When you feel self-doubt creep into your heart, claim that promise. Also, you can change the wording of the verse into a prayer of thanksgiving. For example, claim Exodus 14:14 by praying, *Lord I thank you for fighting for me. I thank you for the strength to be still and trust in you.* Praying as if it has already happened will remind you of God's endless power and release you from the pressure of doing this thing called life on your own.

You have so much to offer. God believes in you. I believe in you. Decide right now that you believe in you!

Embrace the possibilities of this beautiful and messy life. Encourage each other. Love each other in spite of your failings. Trust in God's plans for you. "Let perseverance finish its work so that you may be mature and *complete*, not lacking anything" (James 1:4).

Now you have a decision to make. How are YOU going to change the world?

Acknowledgments

To my sweet Lord for strengthening me with all your power. For giving me endurance and patience and joy. For qualifying me to share in your glorious light.

To my incredible husband who got up at 6 AM on countless mornings to hear my rough drafts and correct my mismatched idioms. You are my strength, my reason. Thank you for showing me what loving someone really means.

Thank you to my beautiful children who inspire me every day with their boundless enthusiasm and endless love; I know you will be world changers.

There wouldn't be a story to tell without my incredible parents who showed me that, "It's kind of fun to do the impossible." You are a constant source of inspiration and support.

To Tess and Shaun, for growing up alongside me in life and business and teaching me that no dream is too big and life is *always* an adventure.

My beautiful friends, you have walked alongside me, said endless prayers for me, and loved me throughout this entire process. Thank you.

Barbara Dee, I couldn't have done it without your constant encouragement. You have a gift. Thank you for sharing it with me.

About the Author

Kate DeSantis is a child of God, a devoted wife and mother to her three beautiful children, and an entrepreneurial partner with her husband. Their company, Hallmark Business Advisors, serves as the catalyst to help married business owners work, live, and grow in their love together. DeSantis spent ten years of her career as the Marketing Director of her family's software business and has seen firsthand the tolls and blessings a business can bring to a family dynamic. She brings a perspective that is both unique and fresh to the world of marriage and business.

She and her family live in Venice, Florida, and she keeps her days full with homeschooling, writing, consulting entrepreneurial couples, and volunteering in her community.

TO CONTACT KATE, PLEASE VISIT

www.katedesantis.com

76183383R00146

Made in the USA
Middletown, DE
10 June 2018